Man by . Pencil .

By

Stephen Peters

ISBN:978-0-244-55705-8

FOR

ALL THE BLOKES

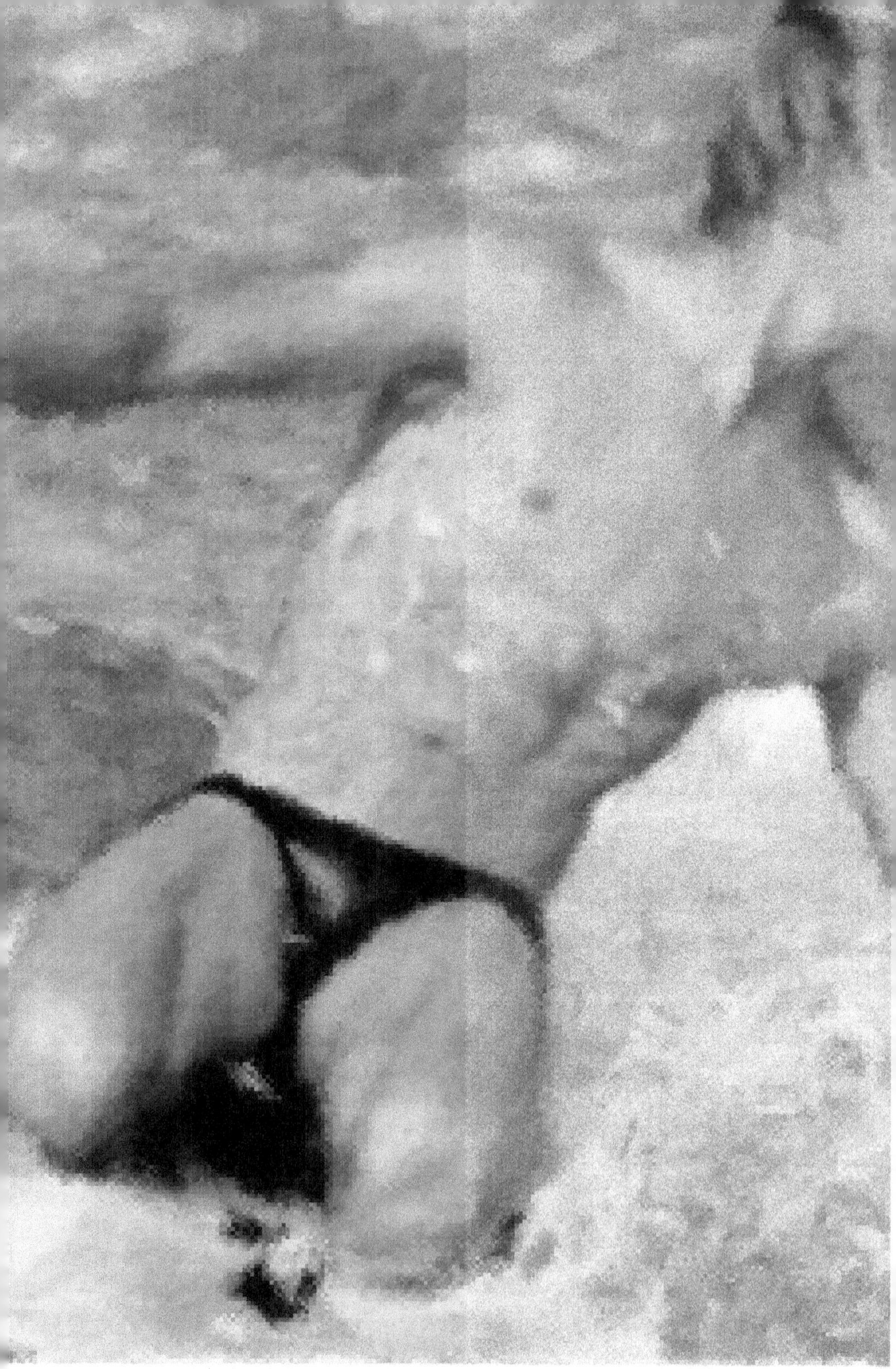

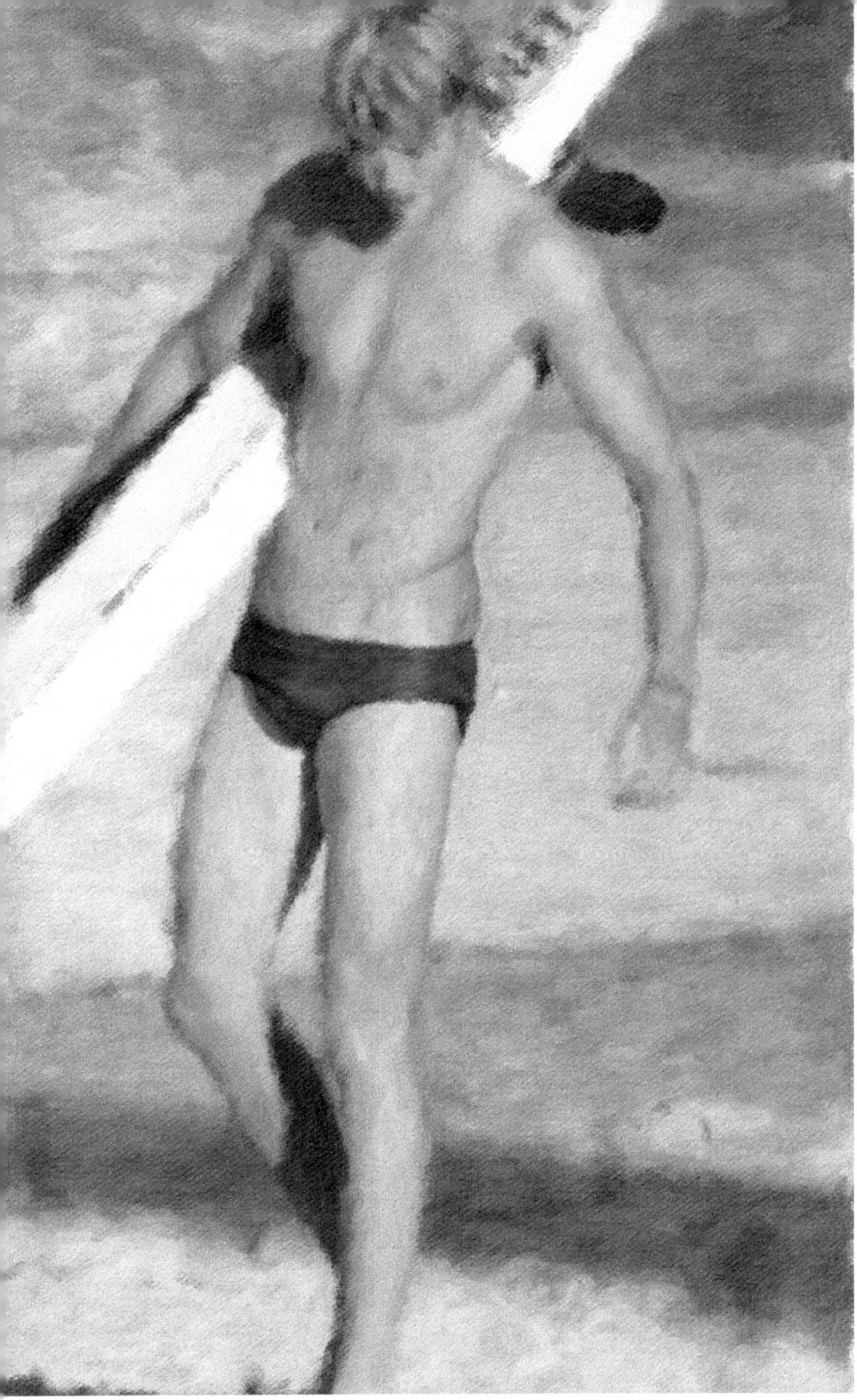

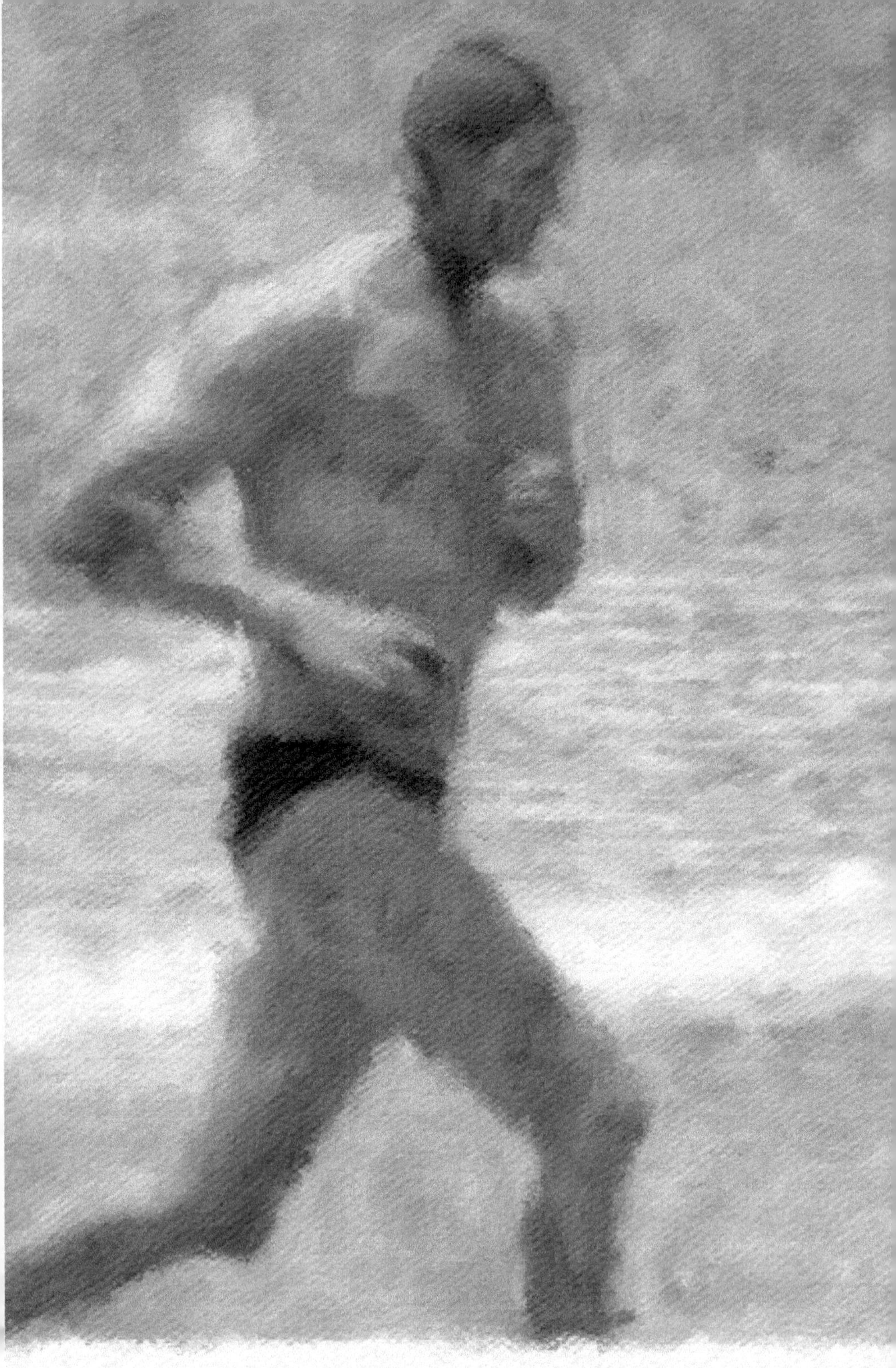

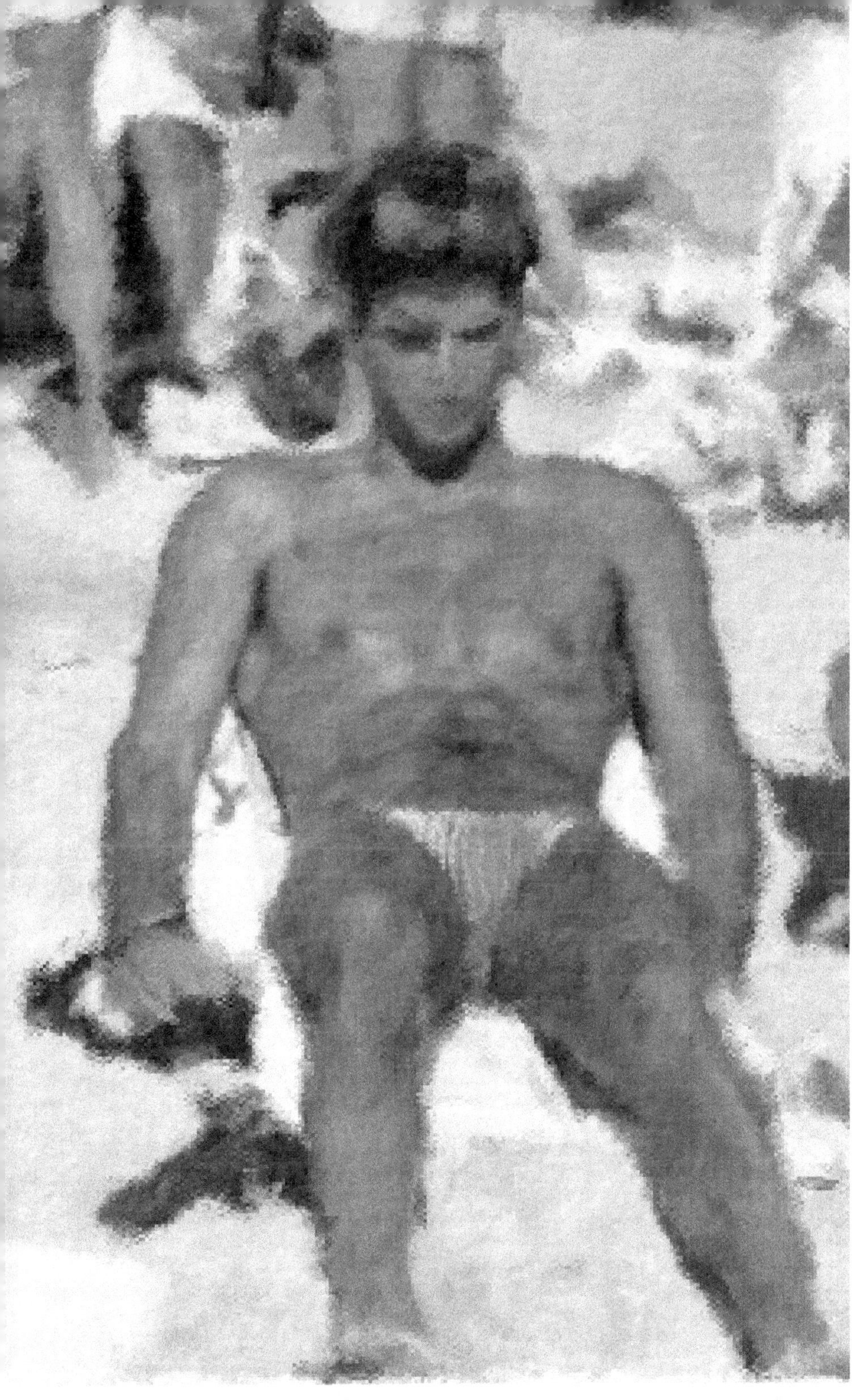

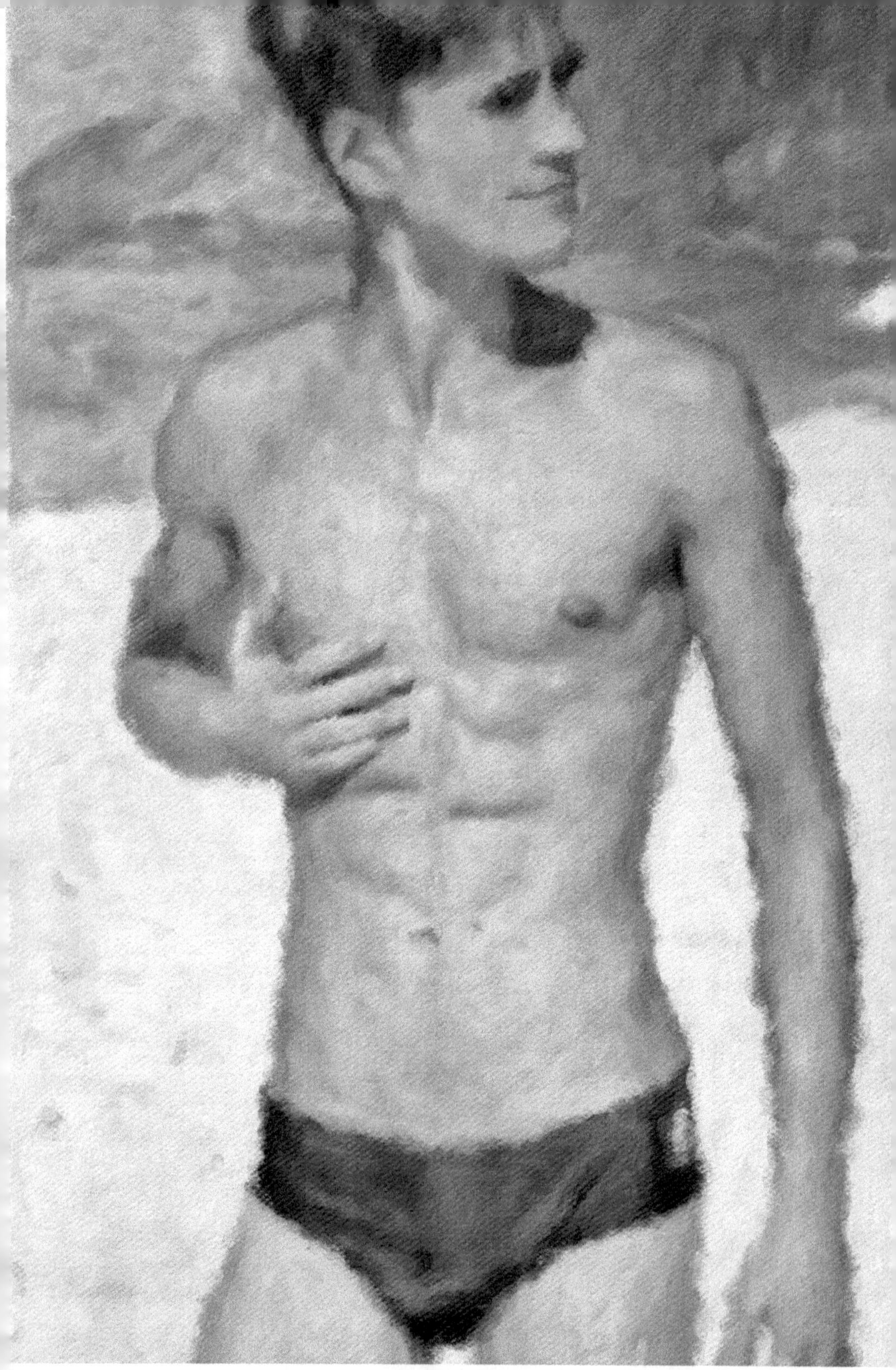

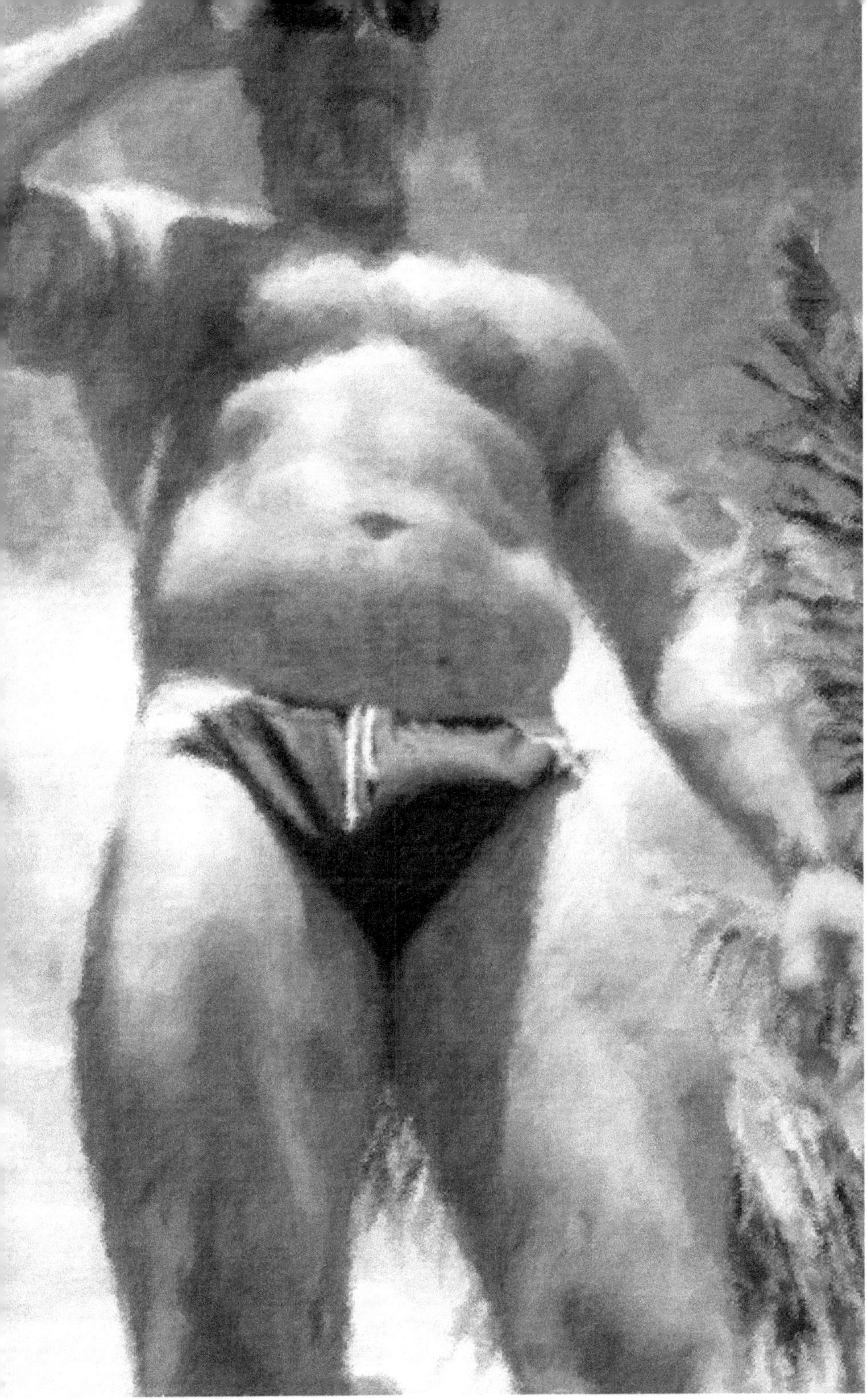

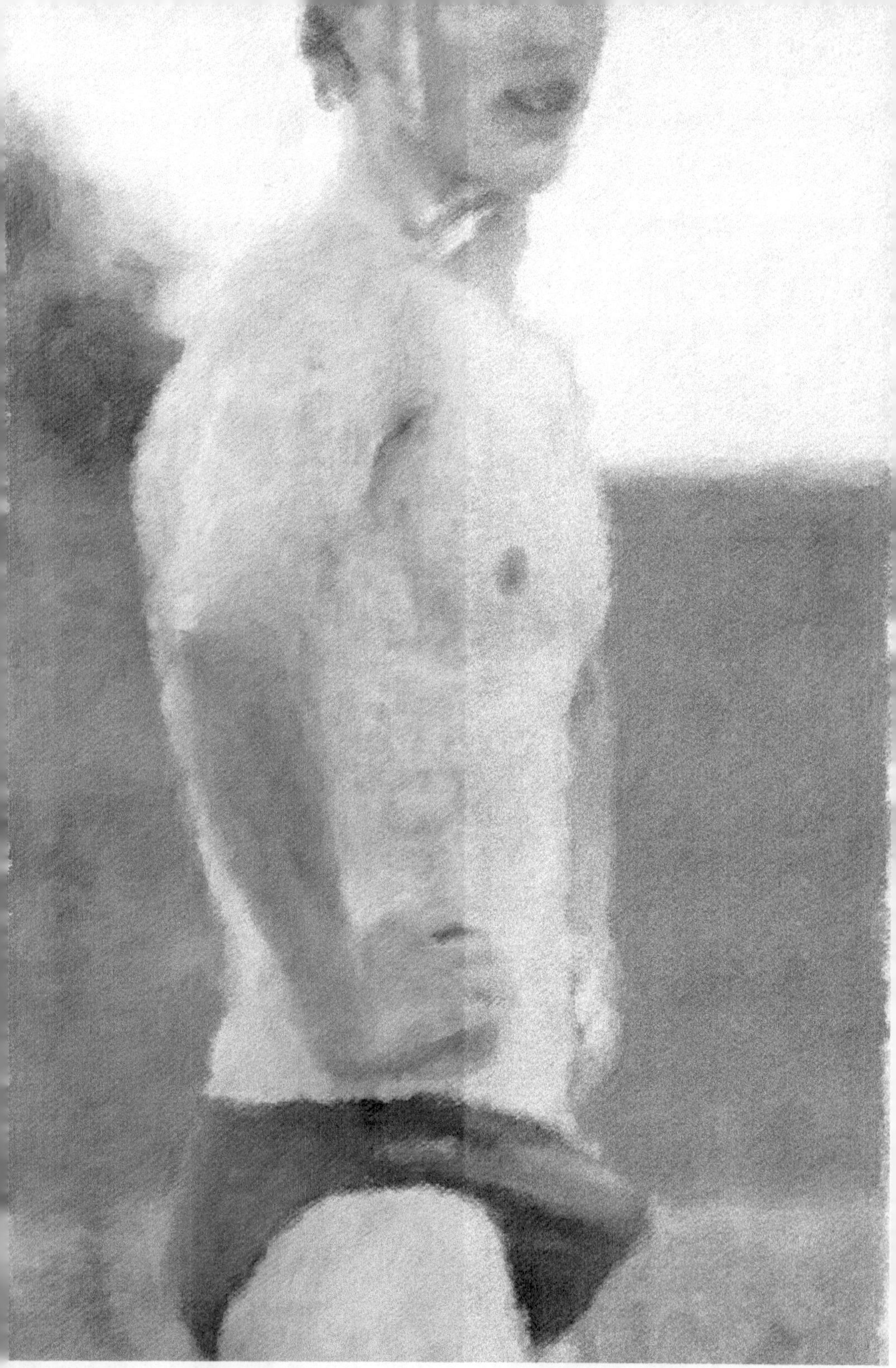

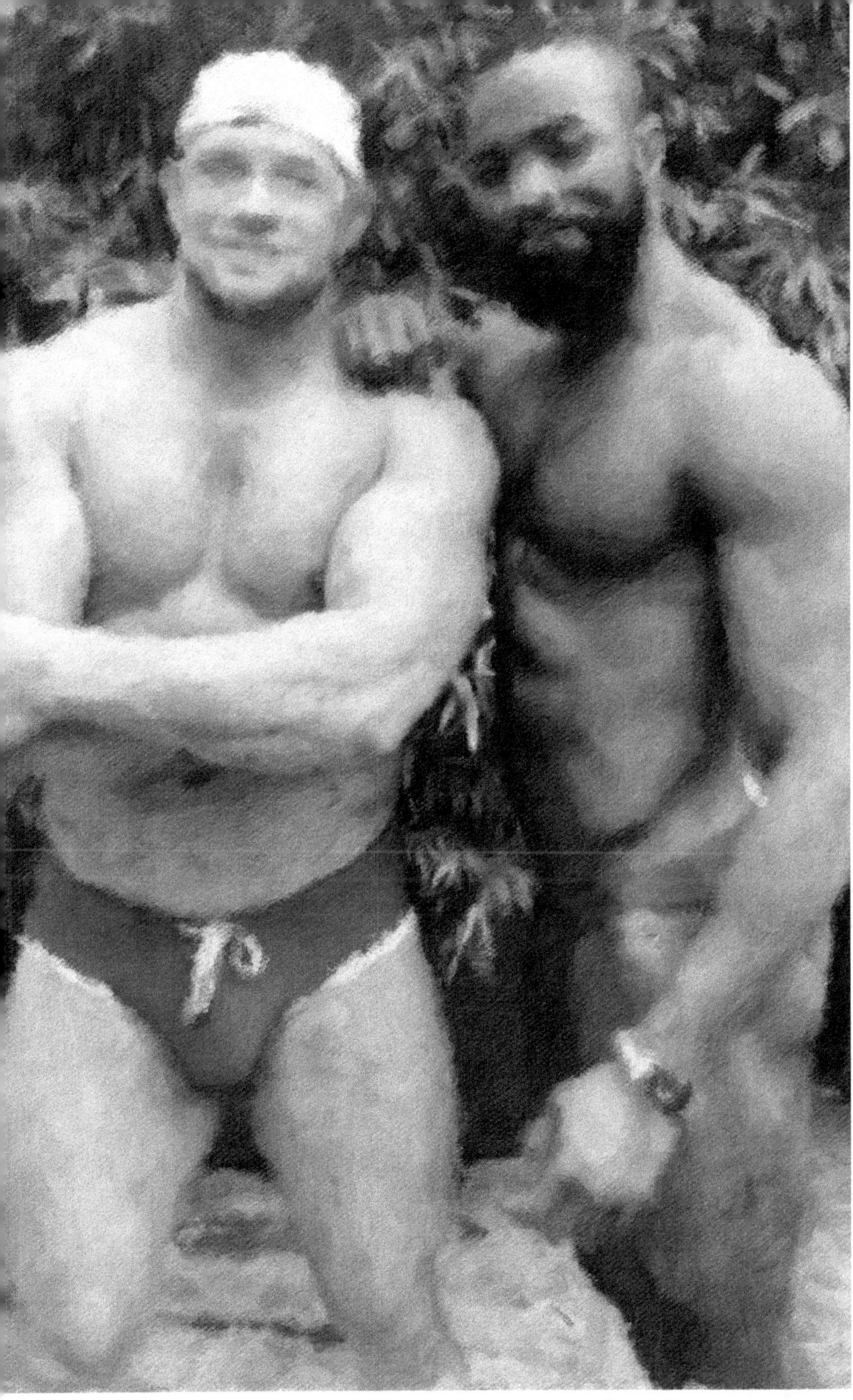

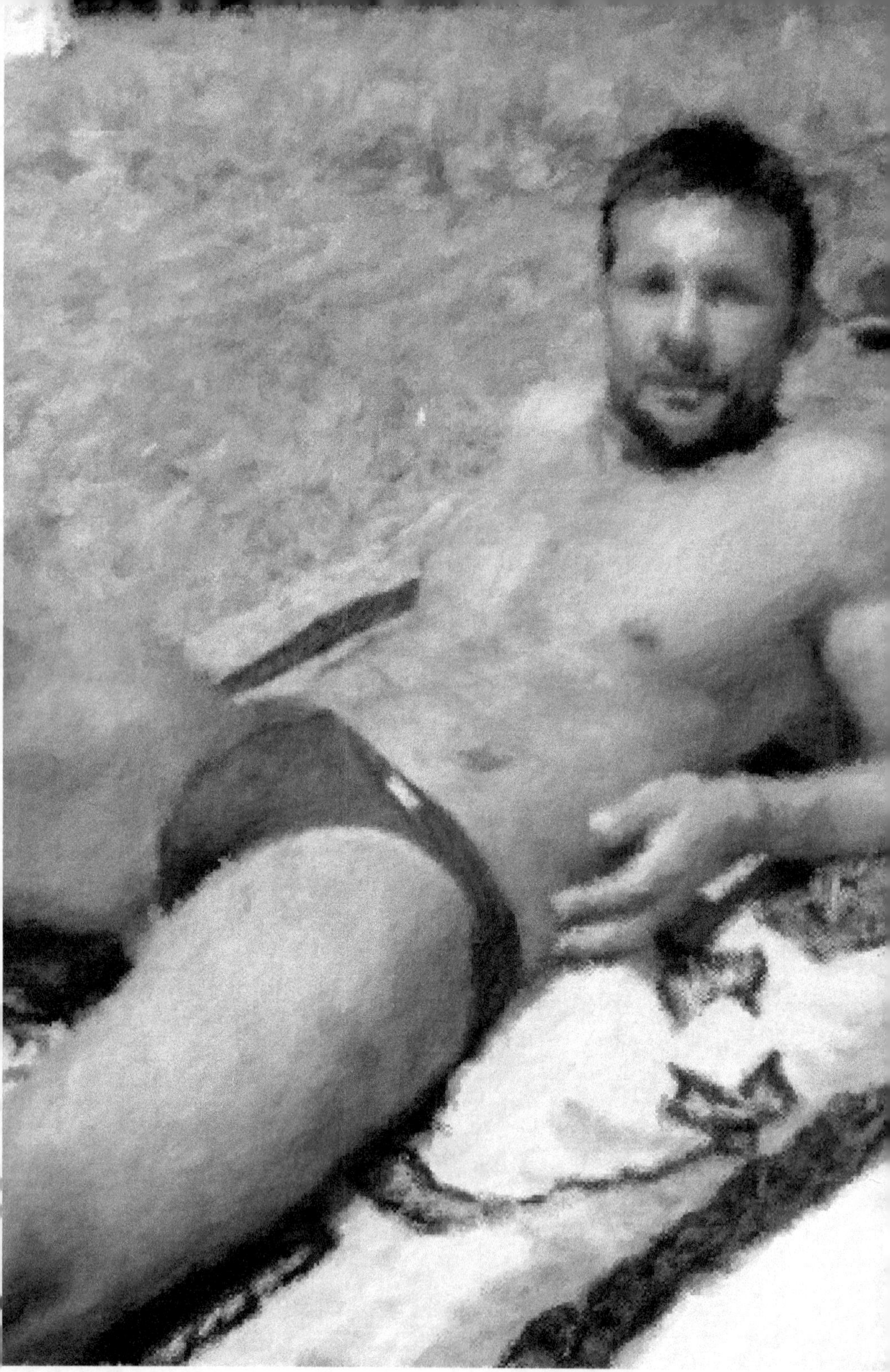

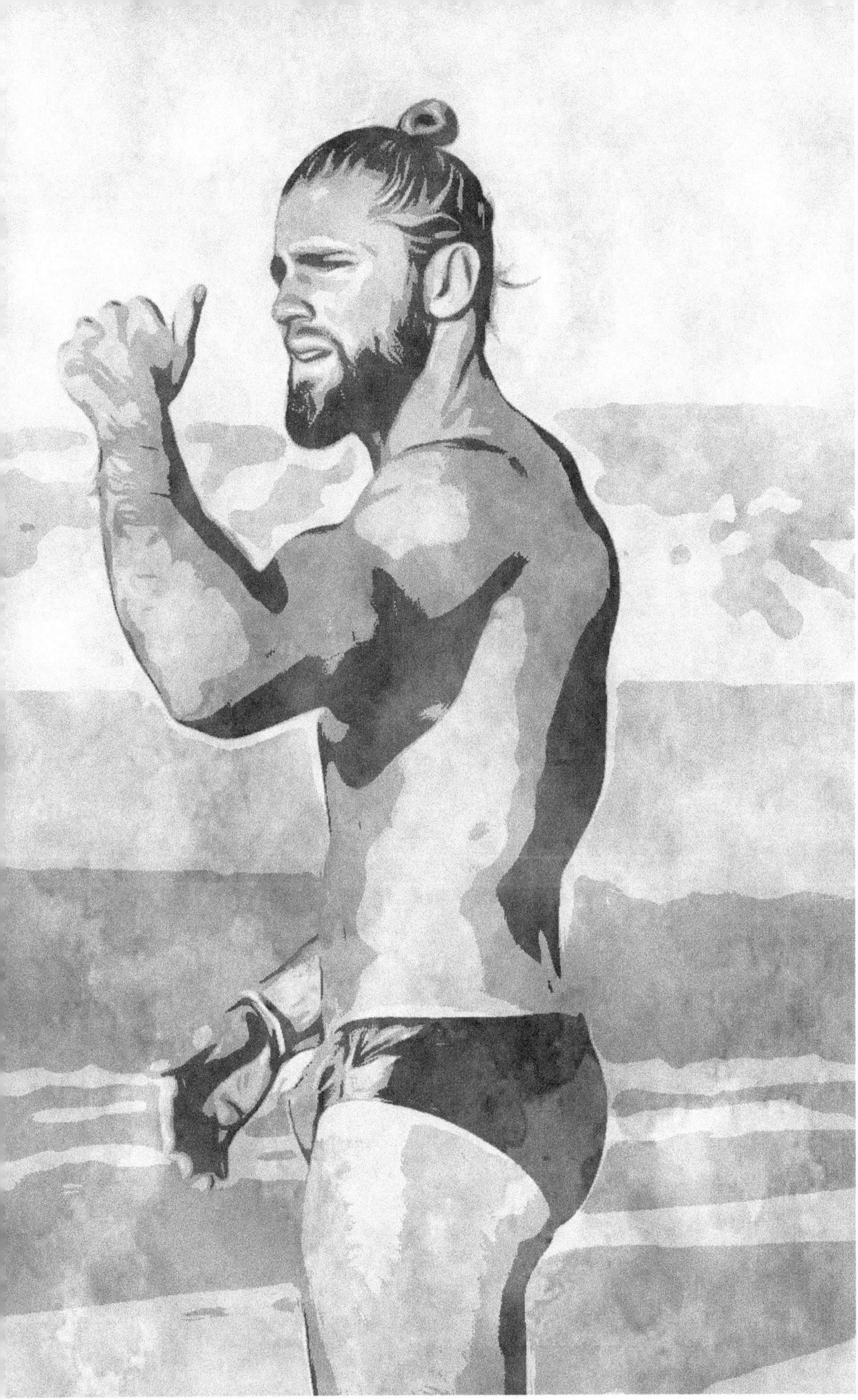

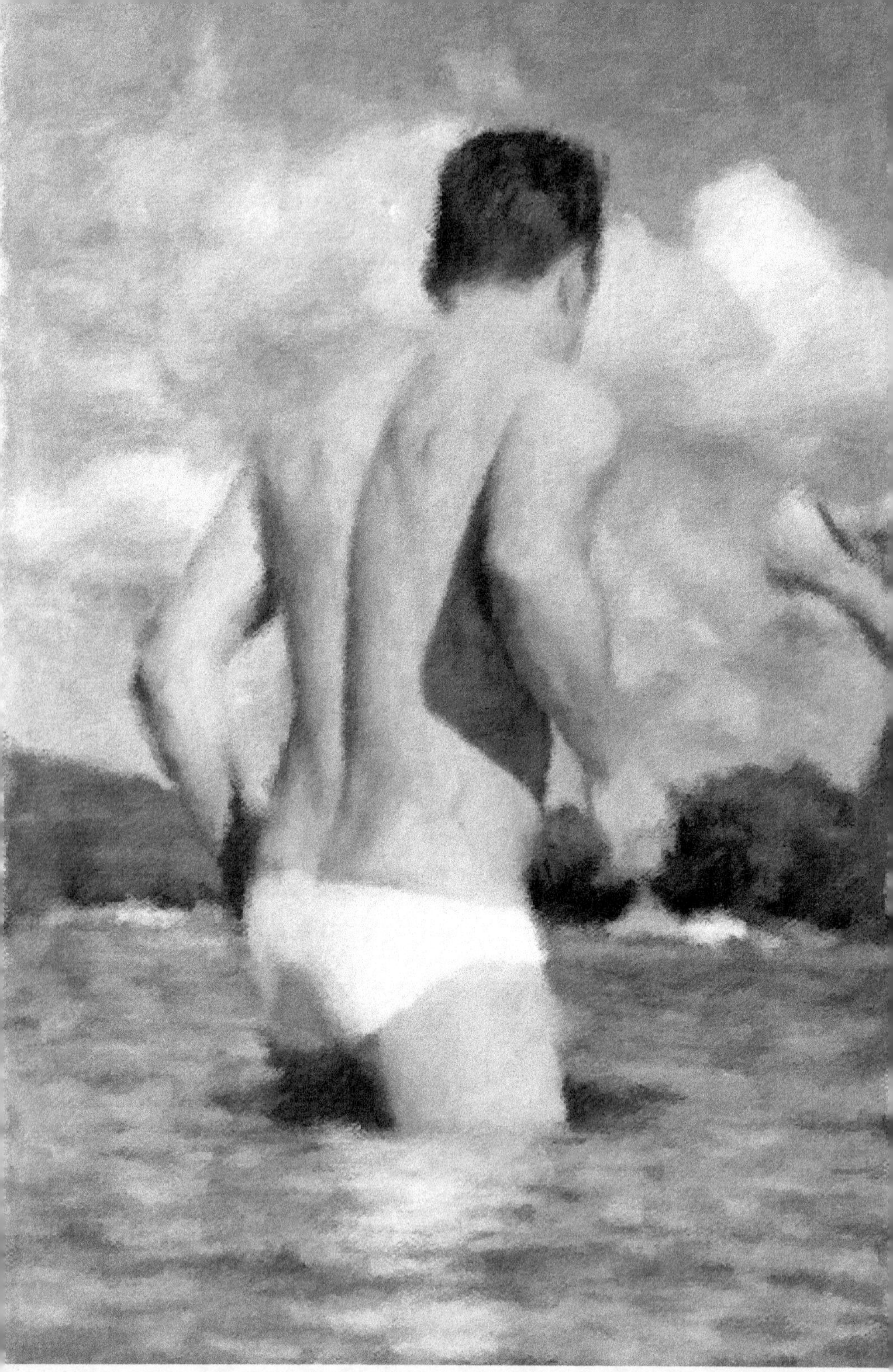

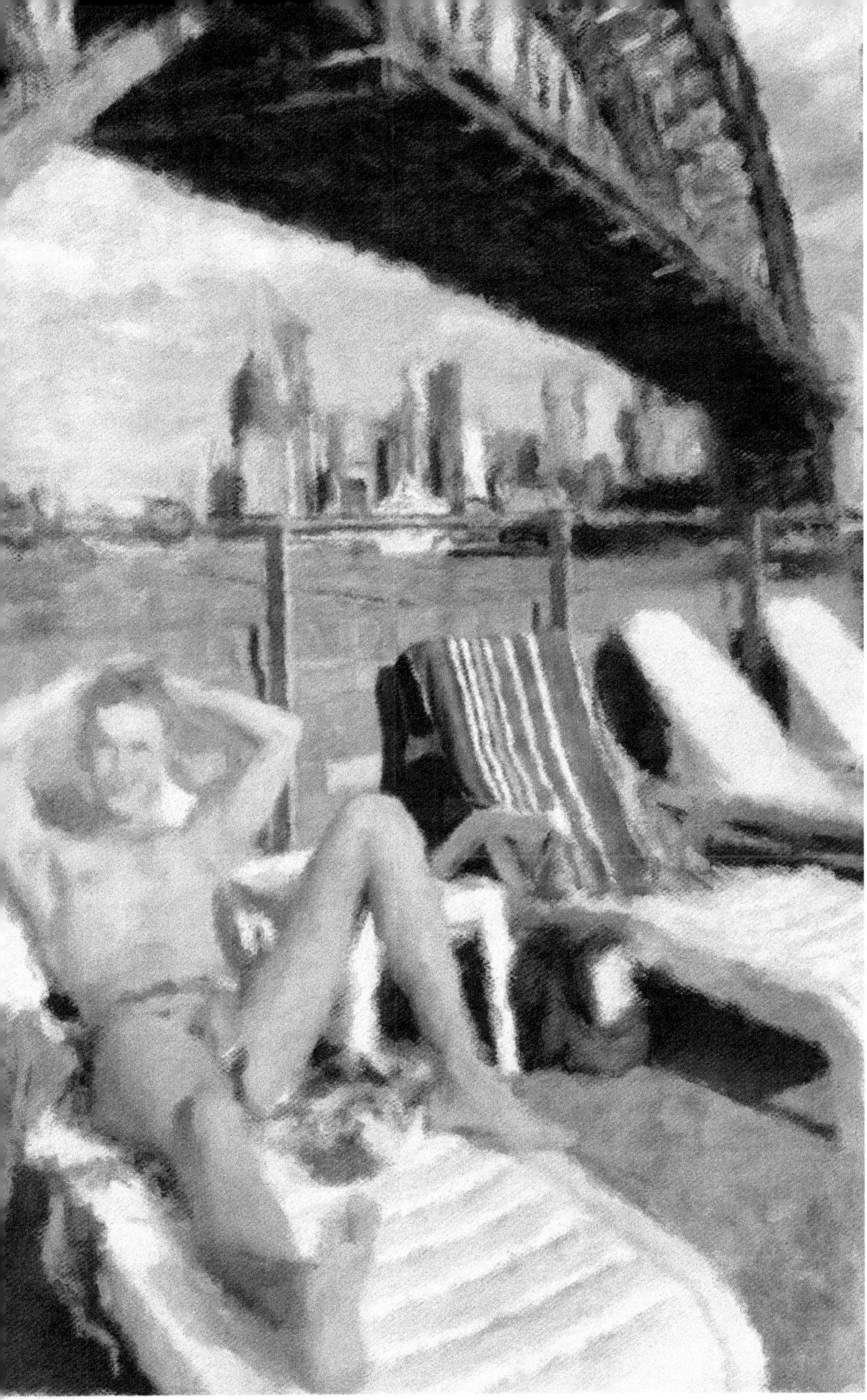

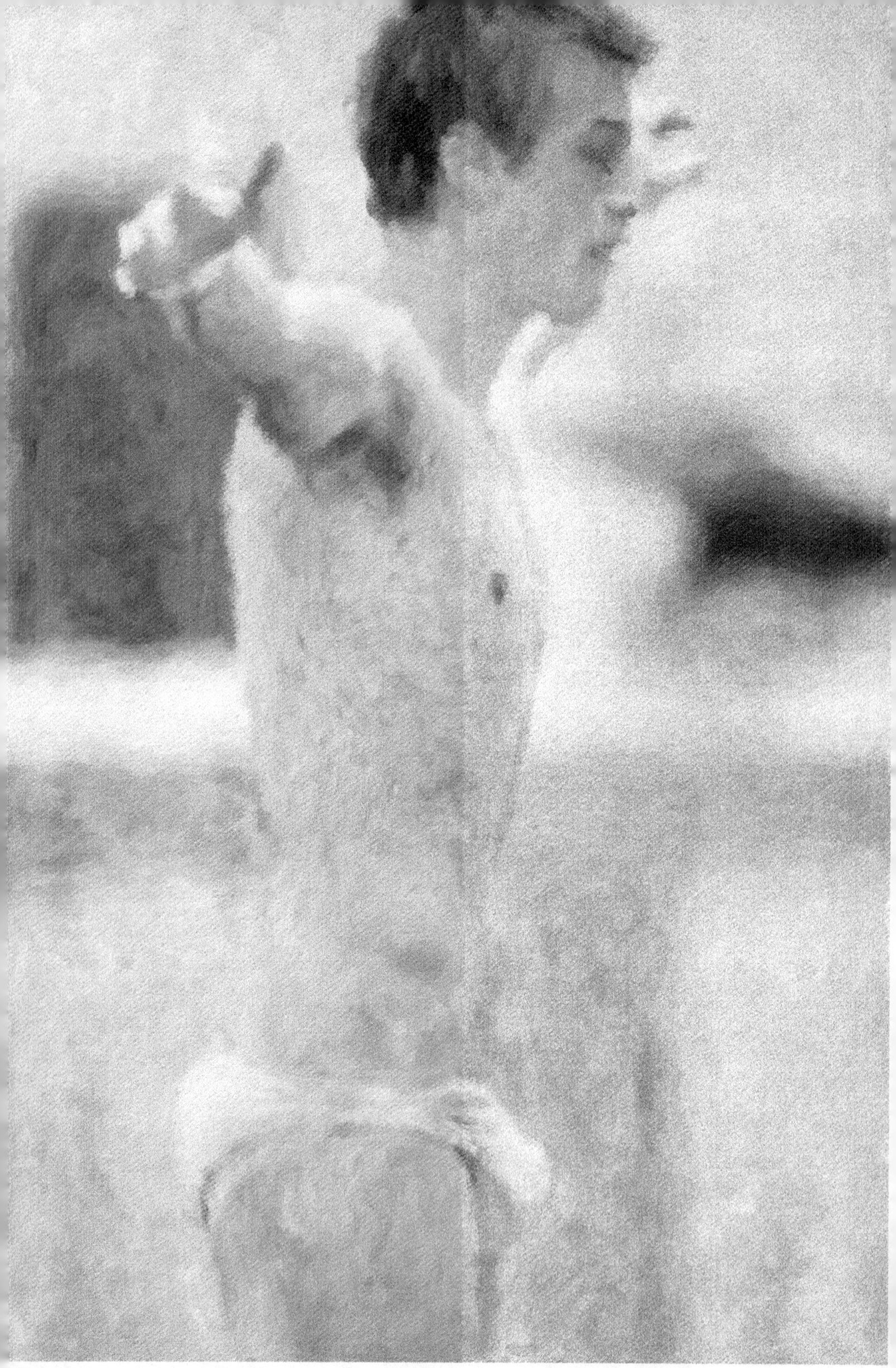

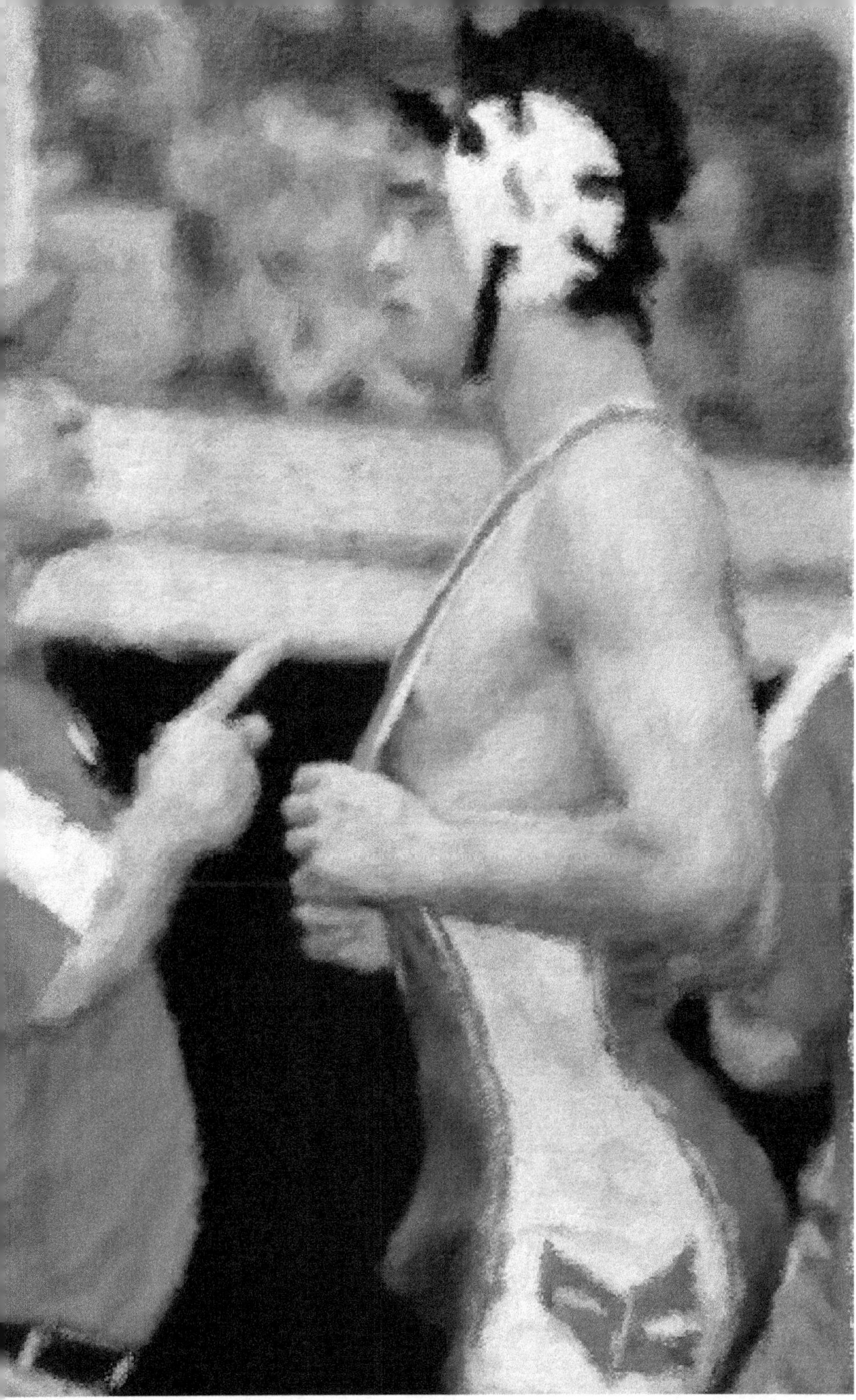

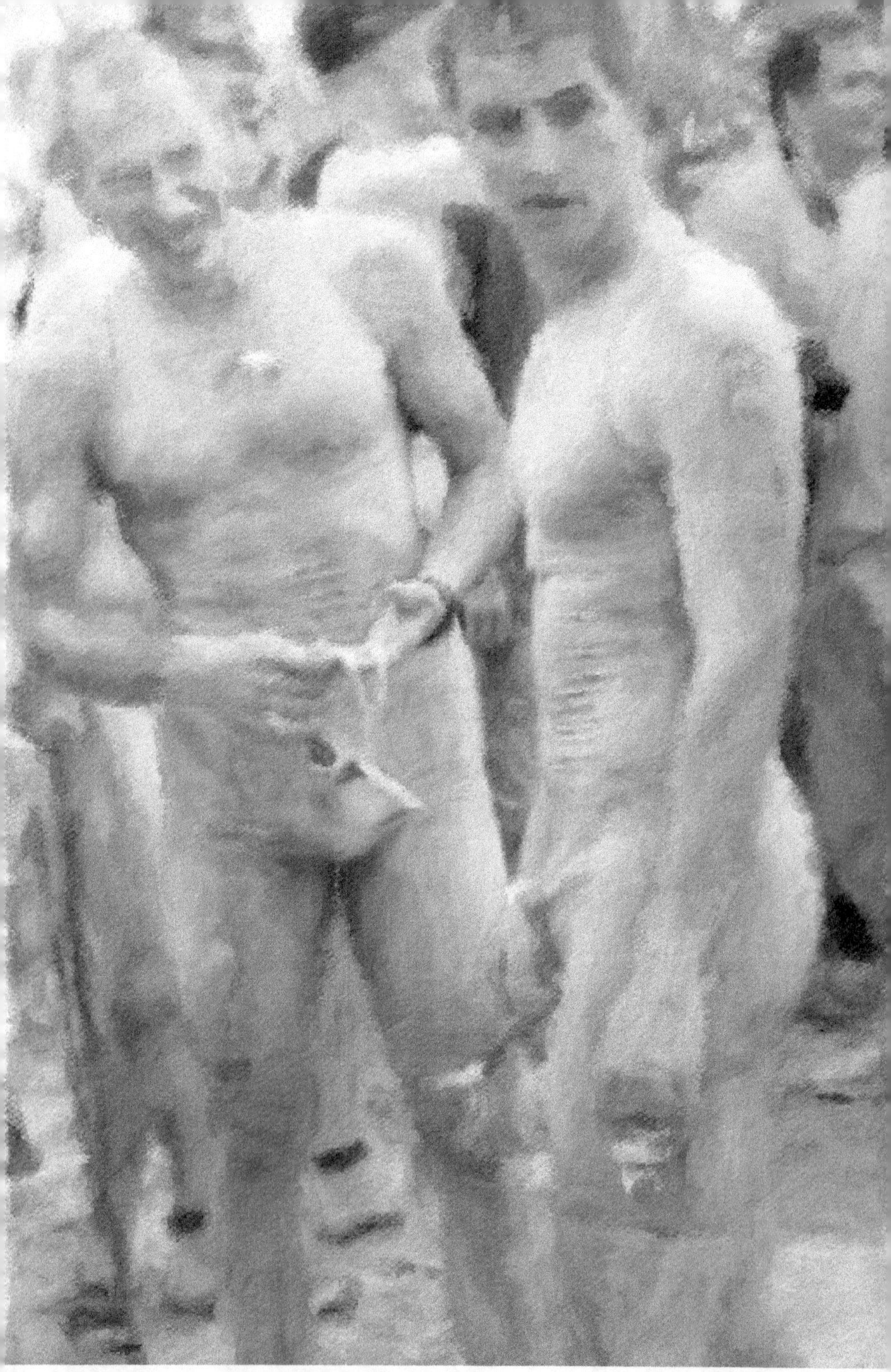

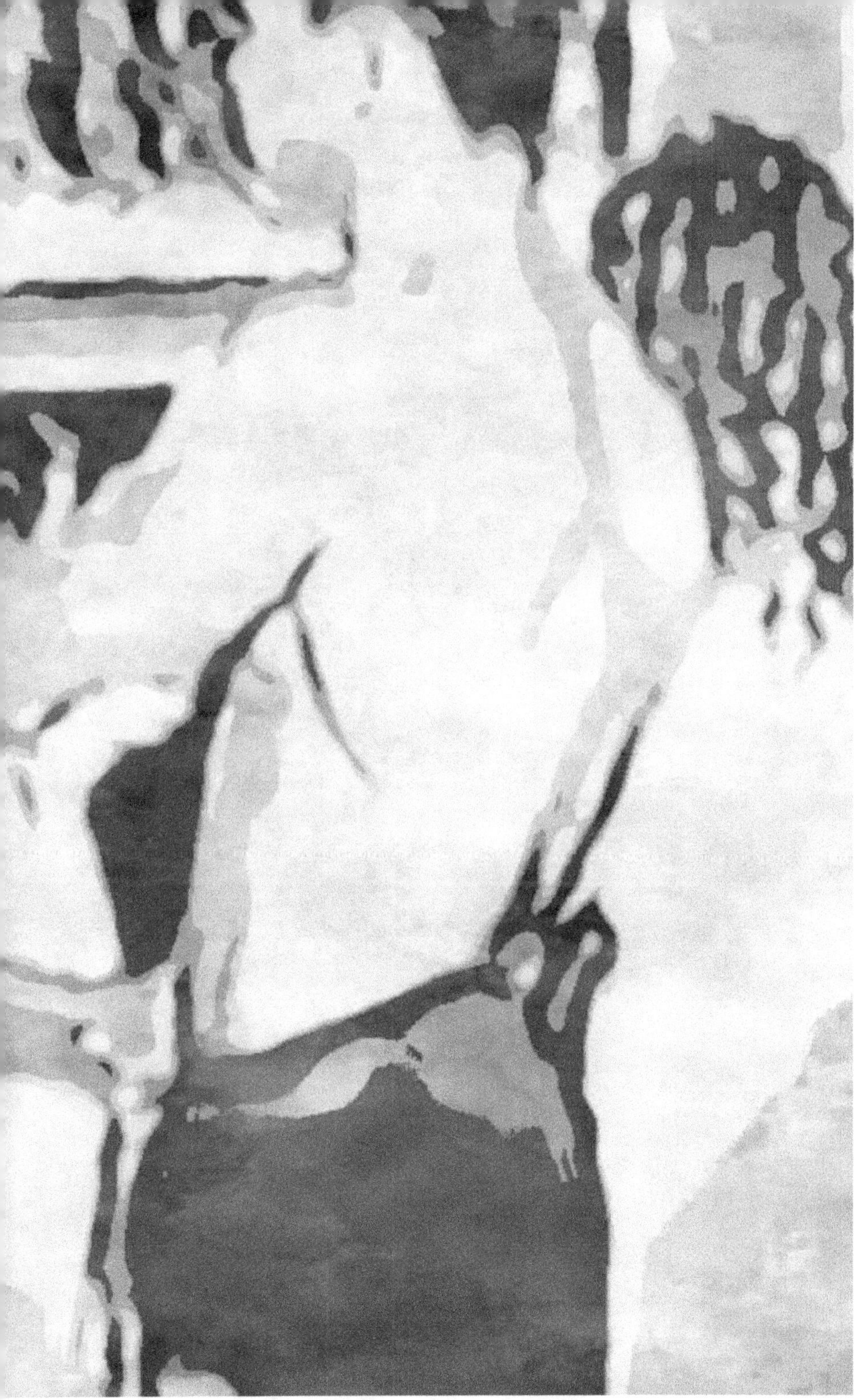

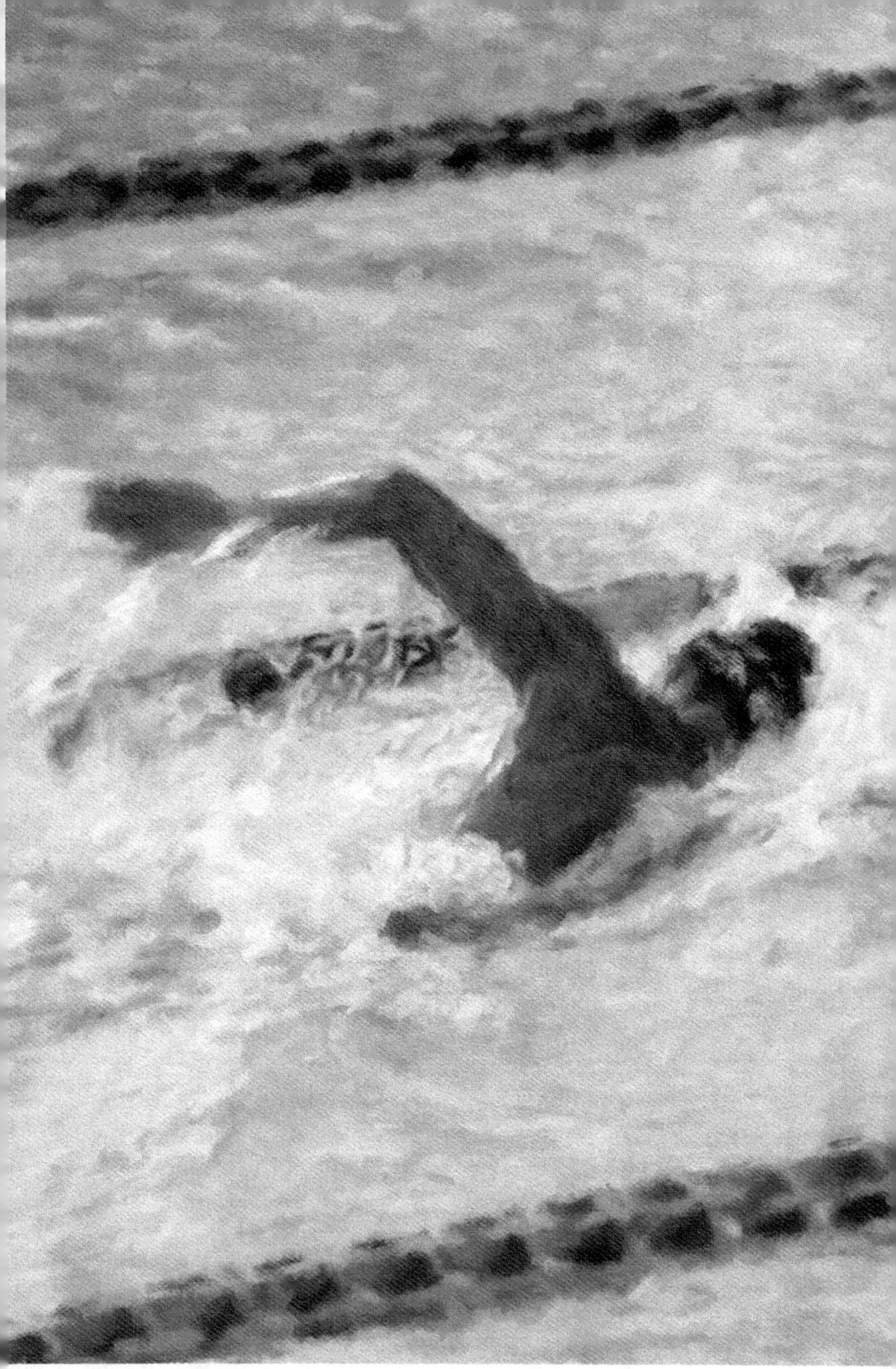

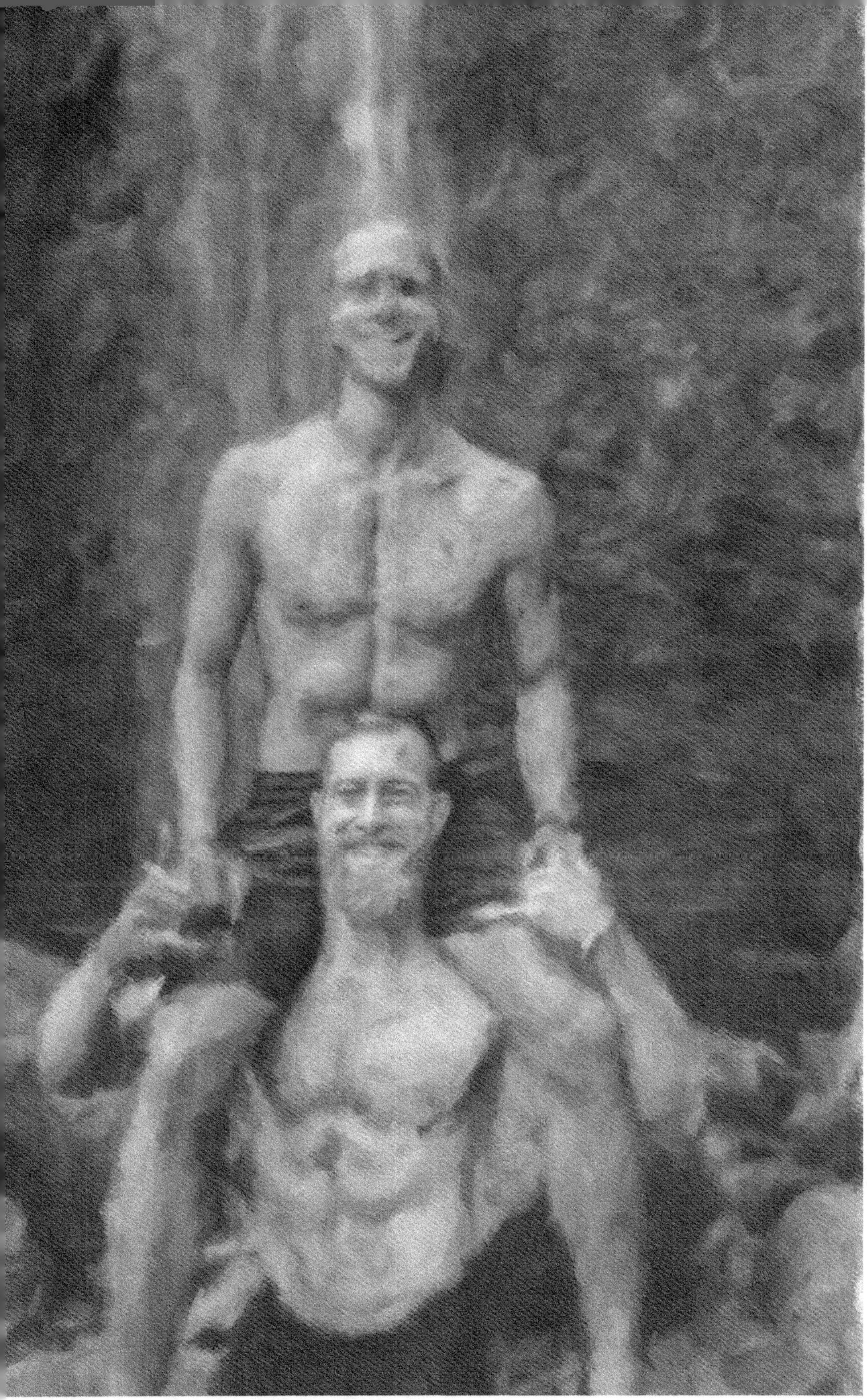

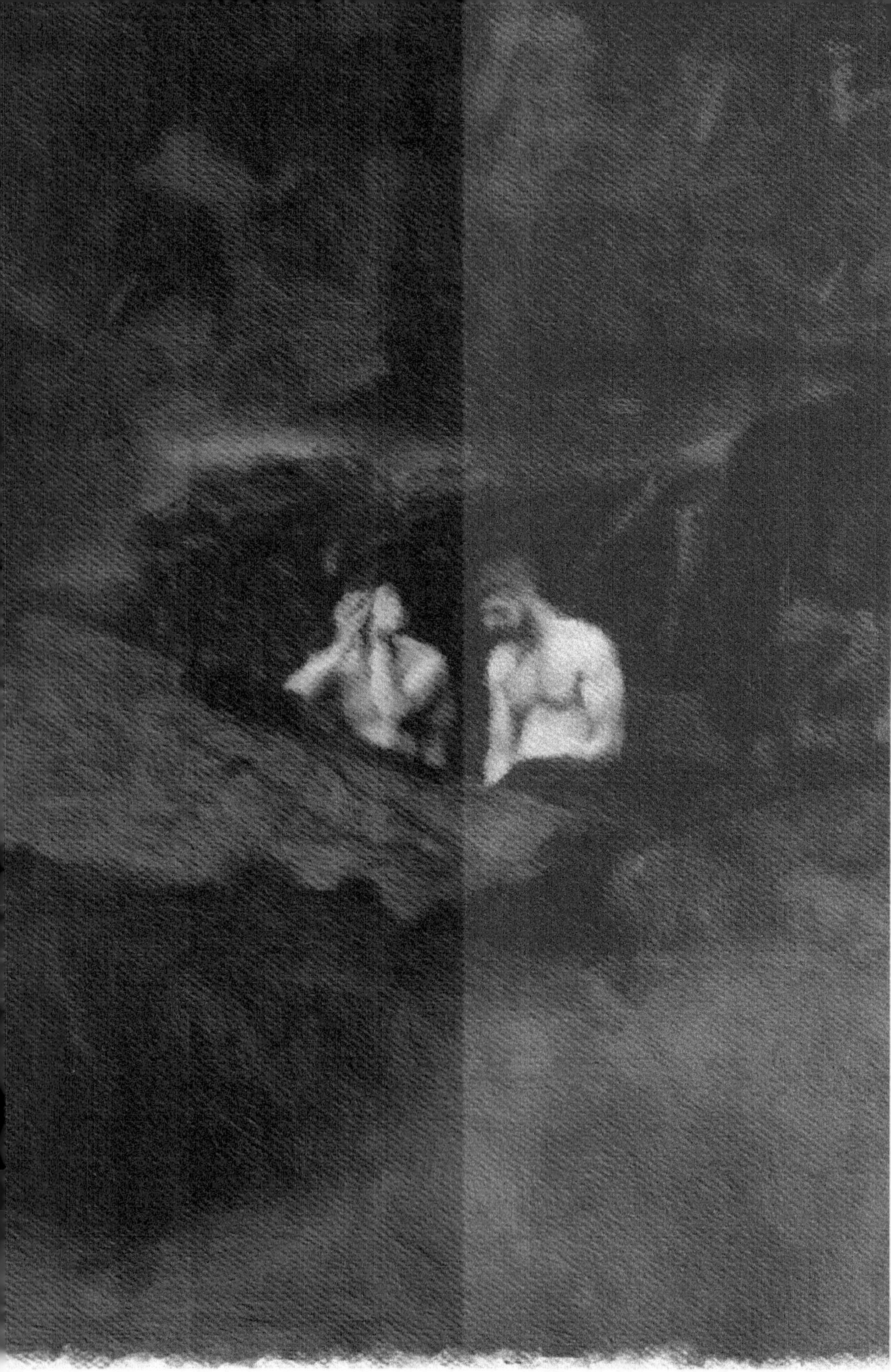

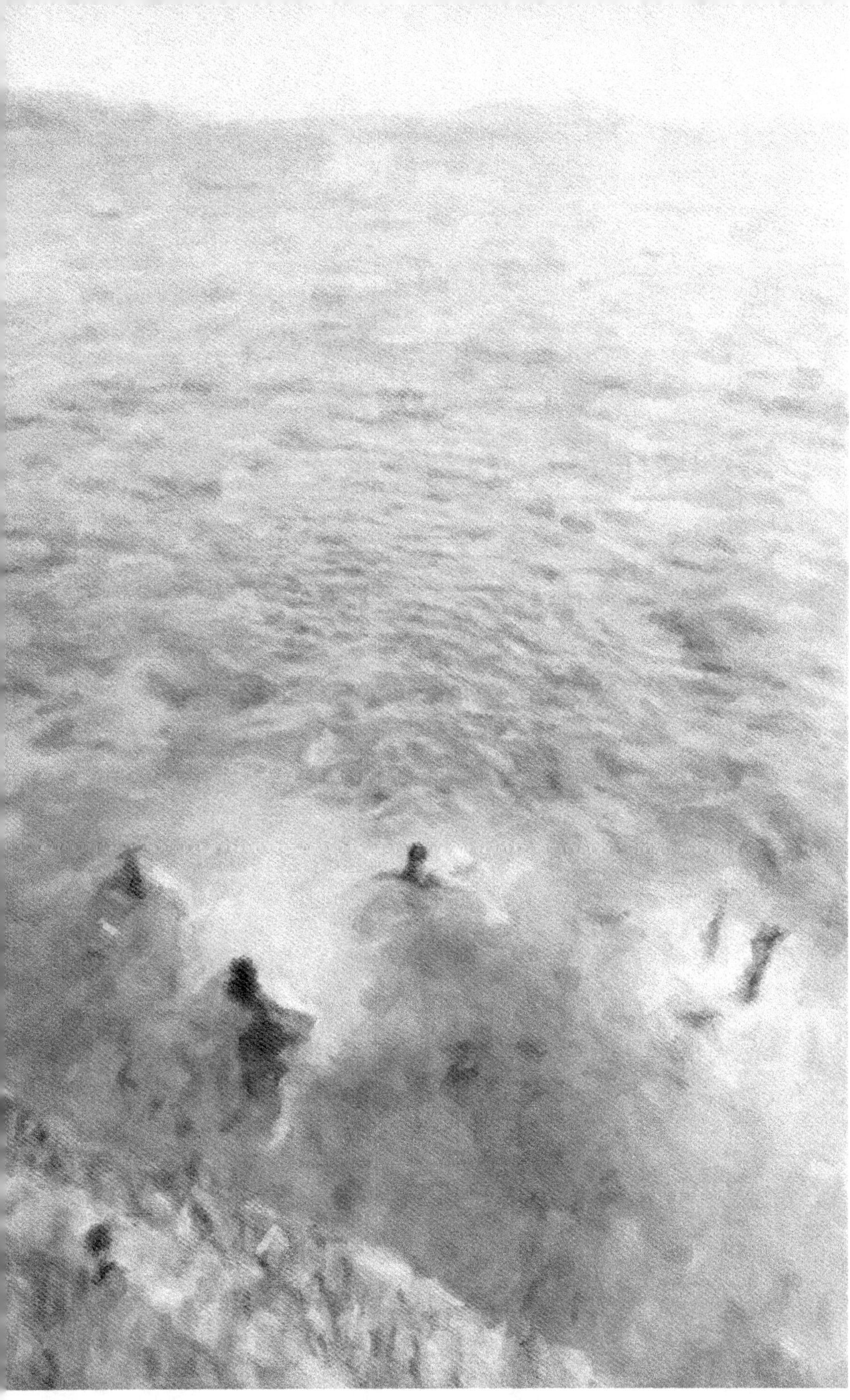

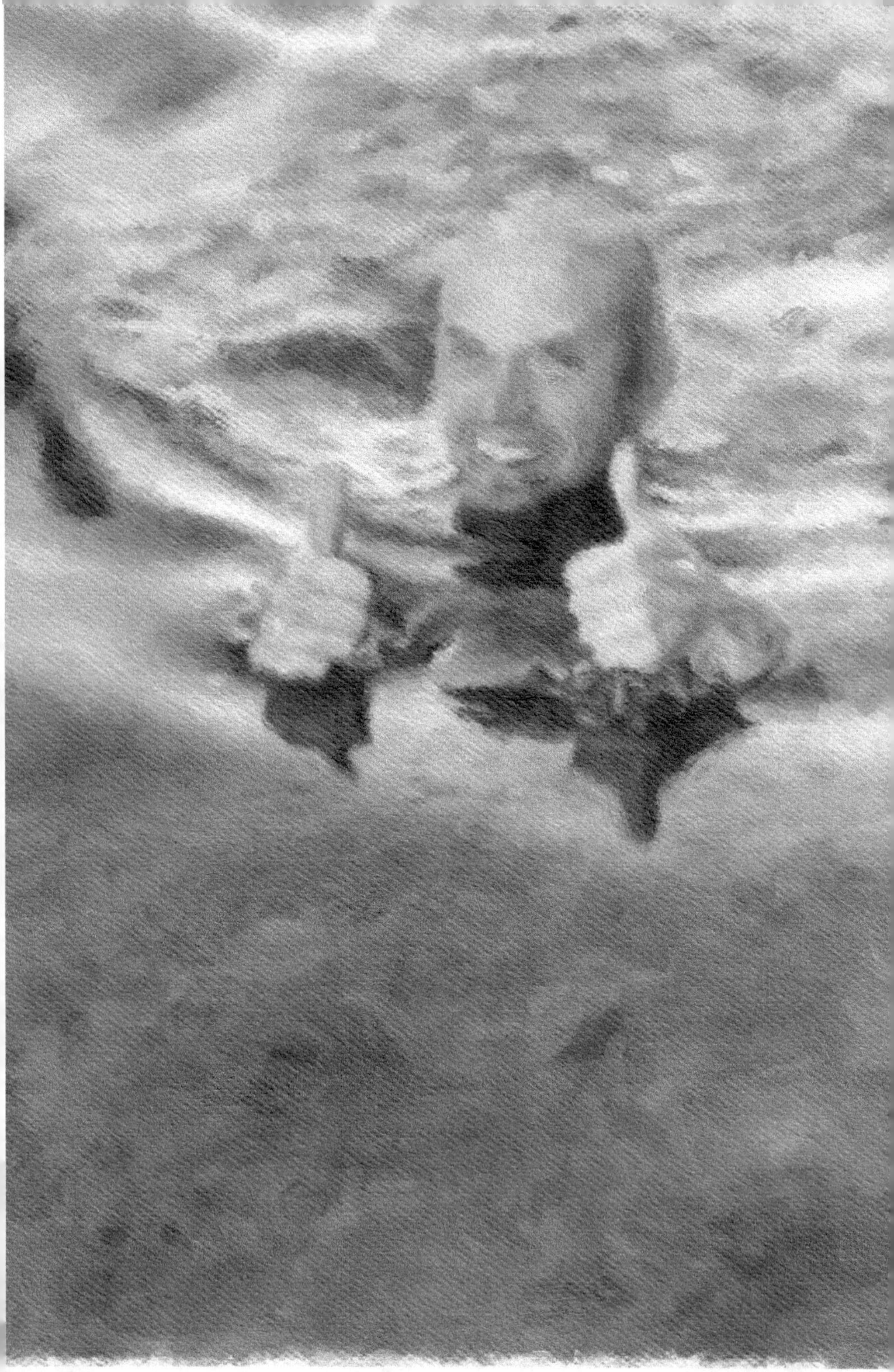

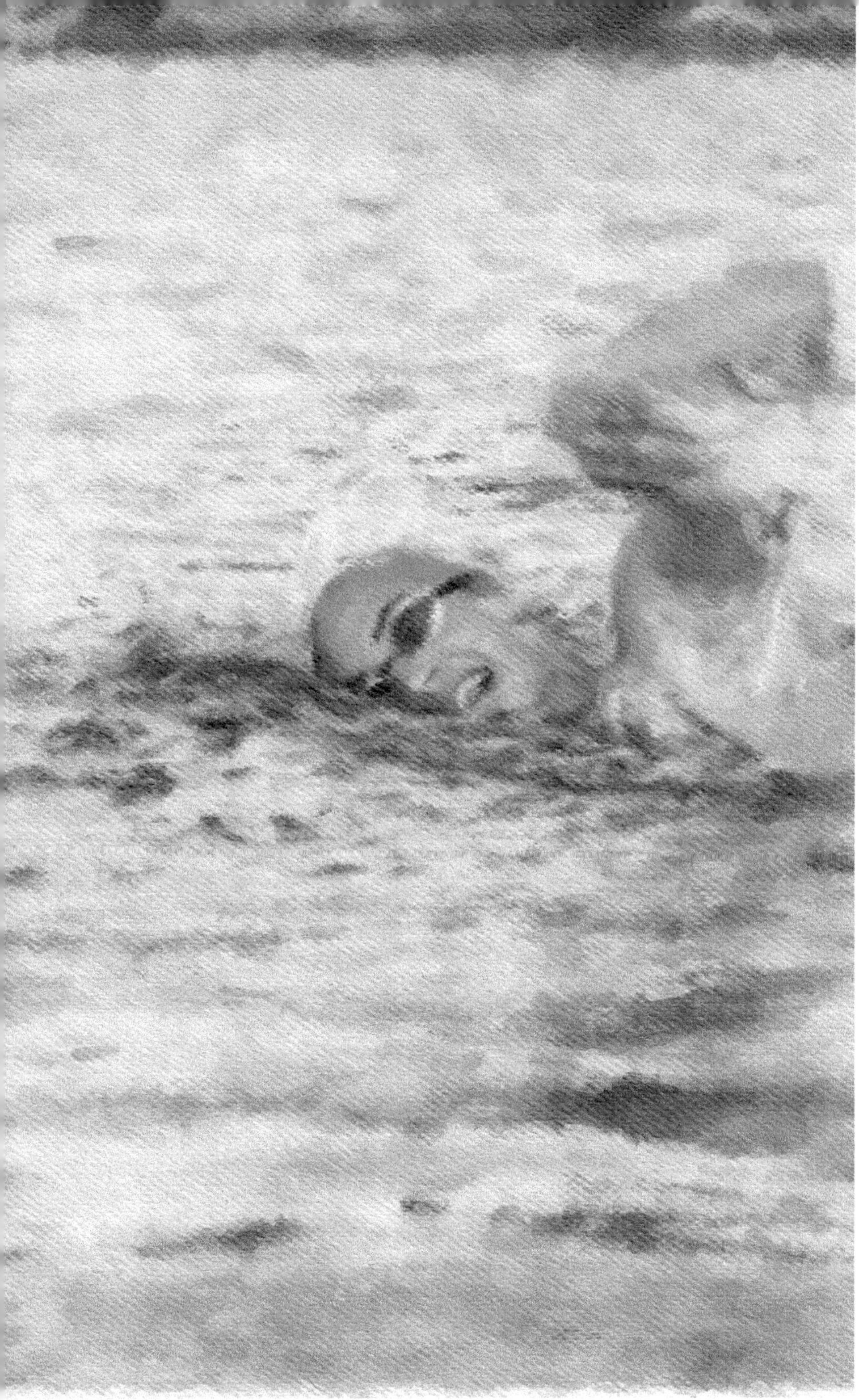

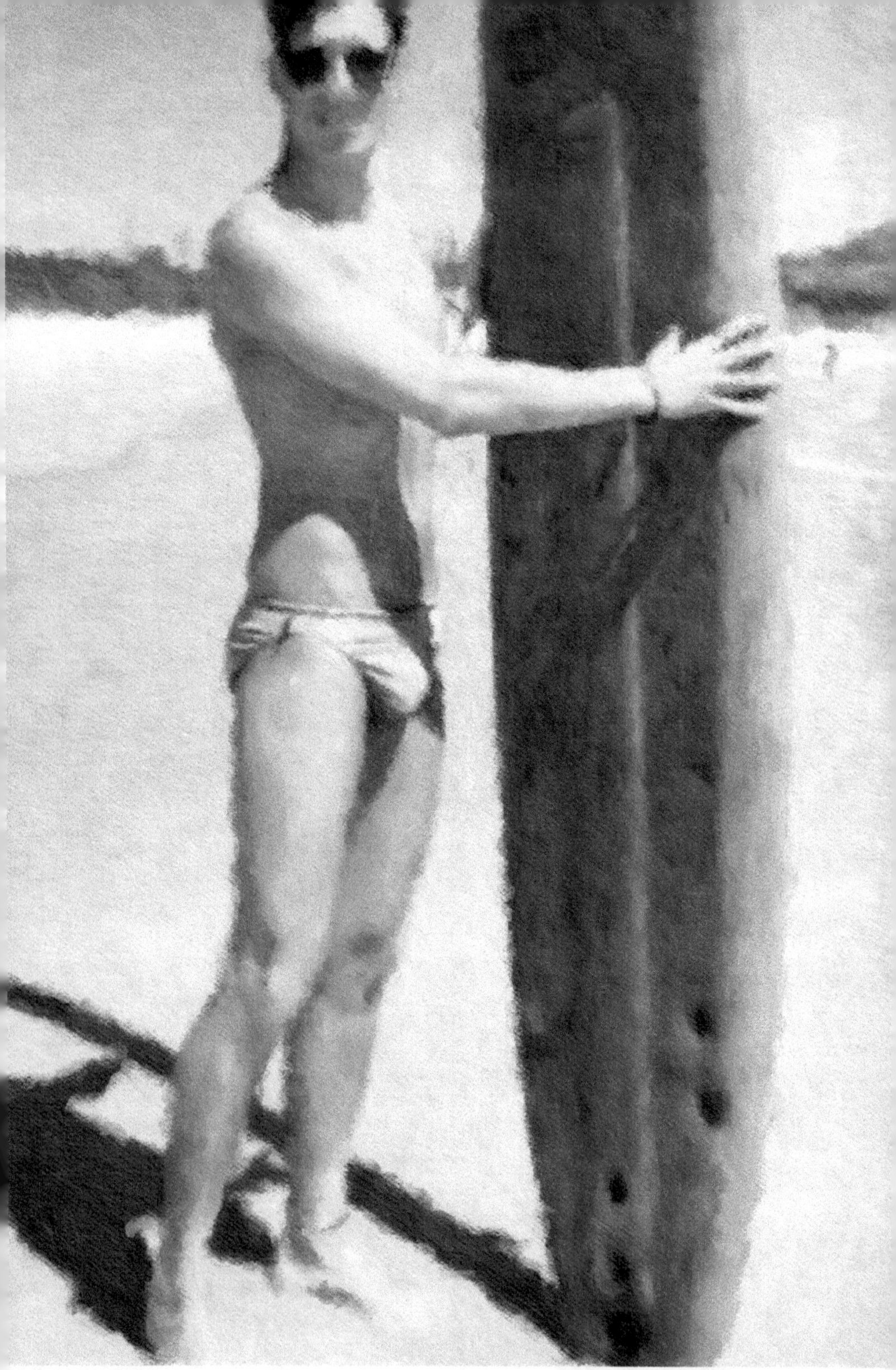

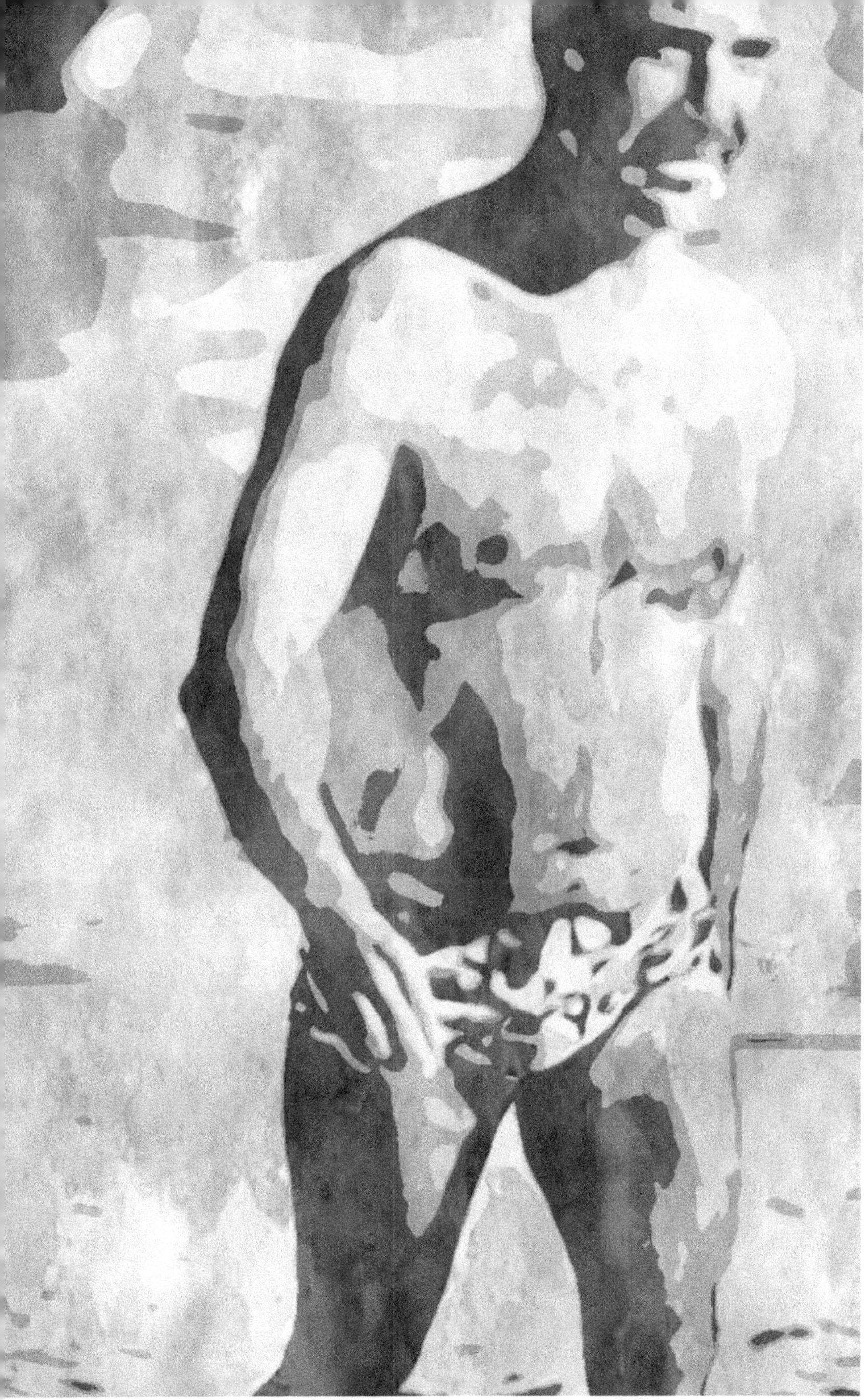

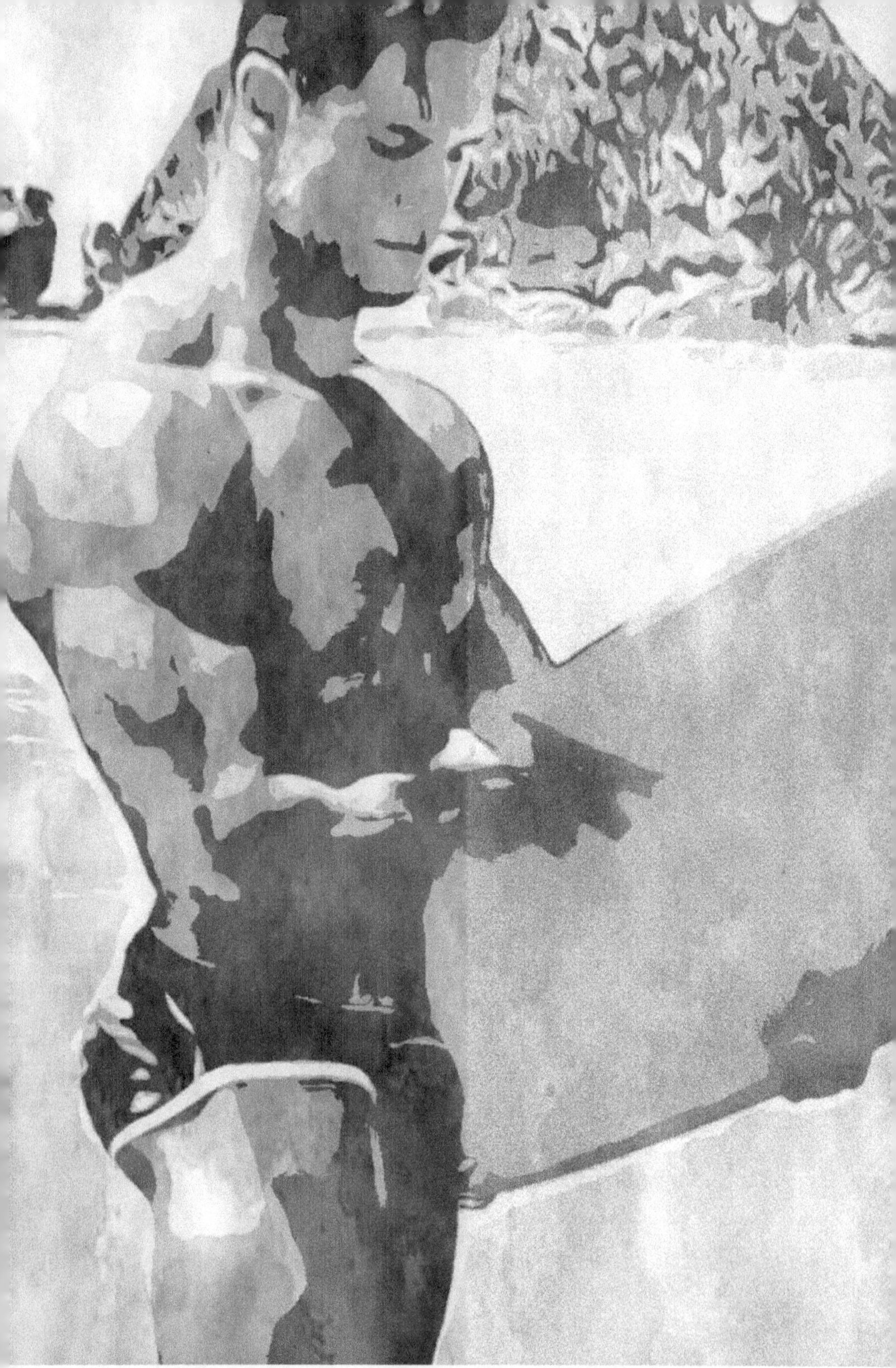

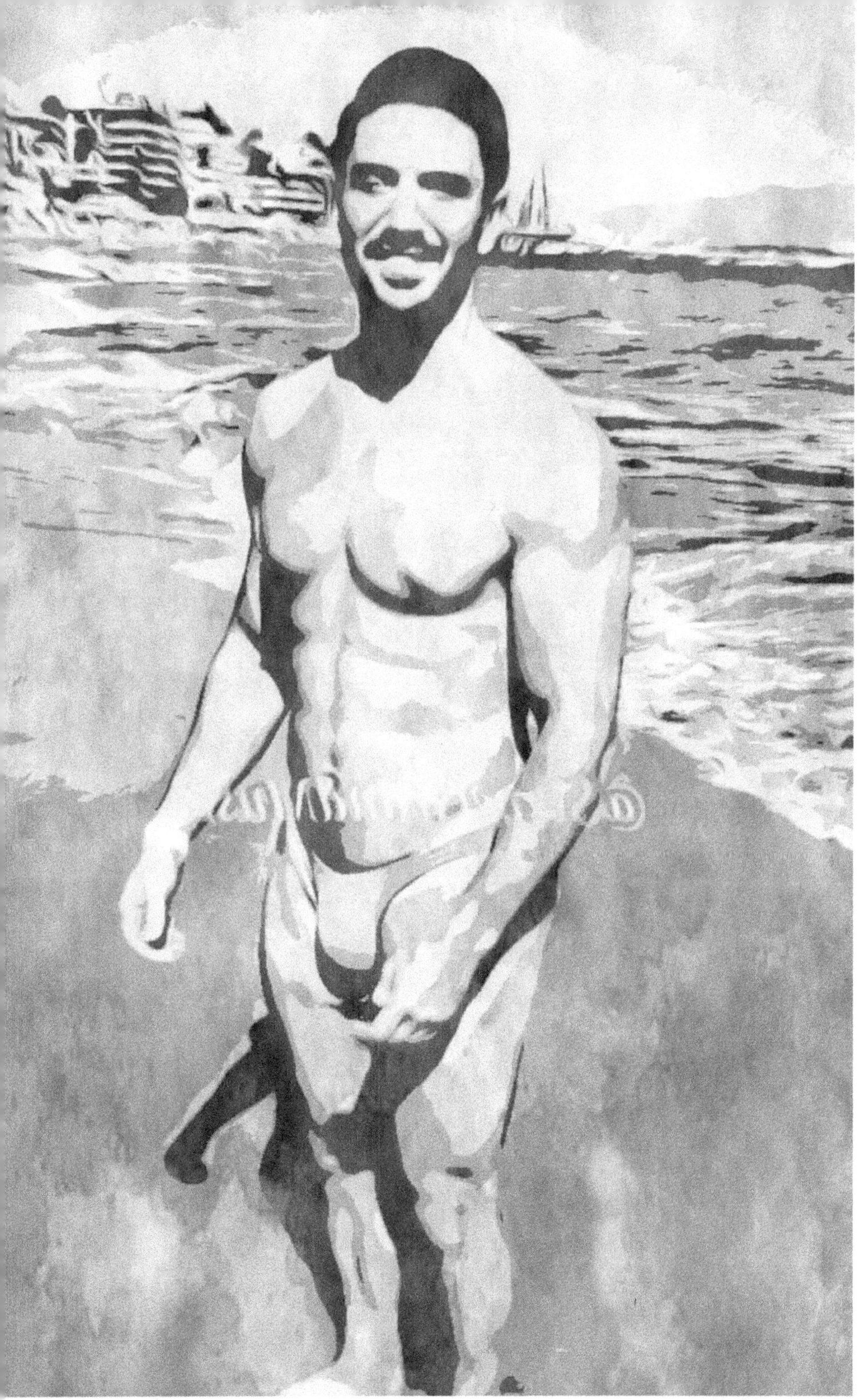

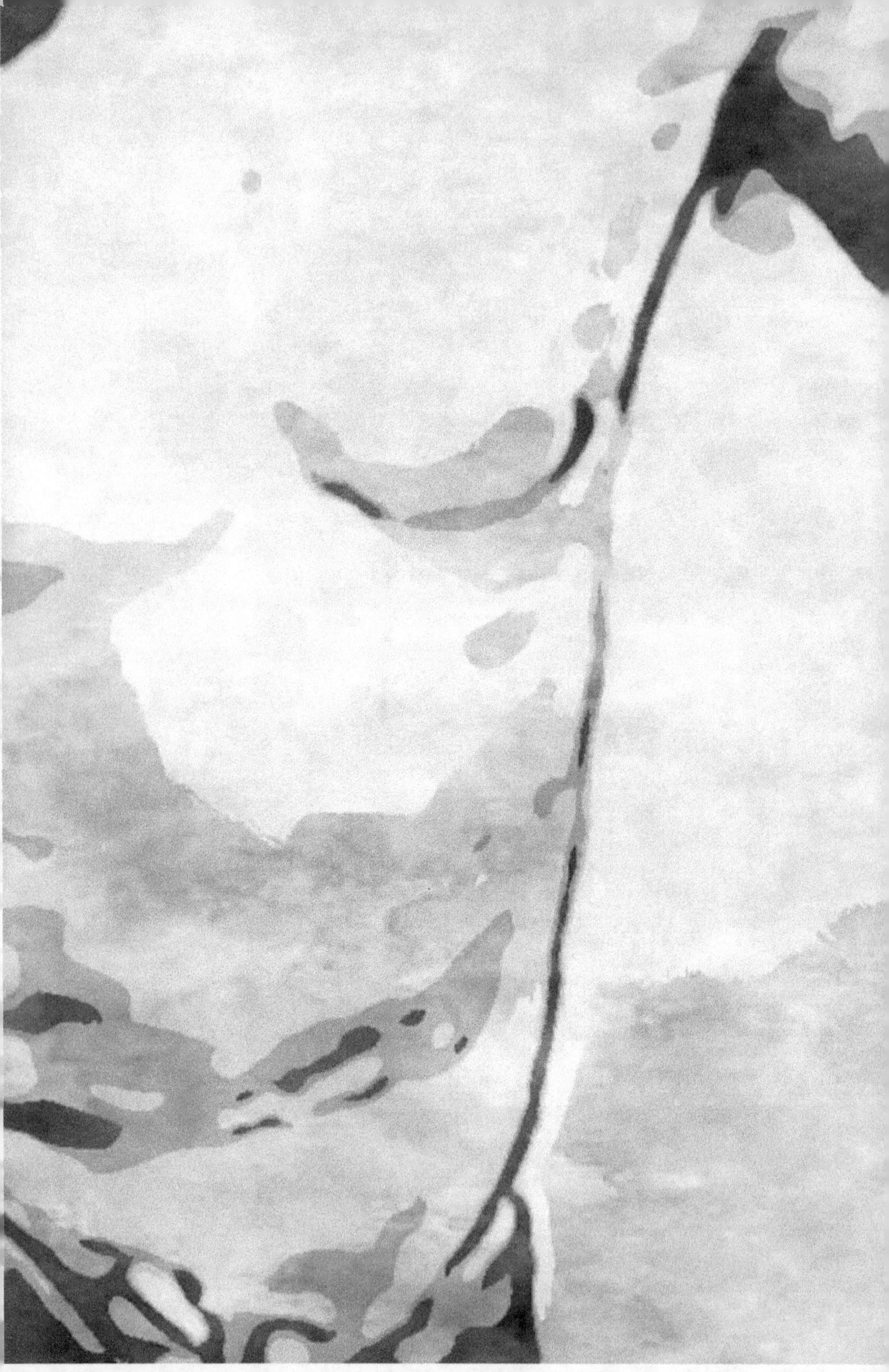

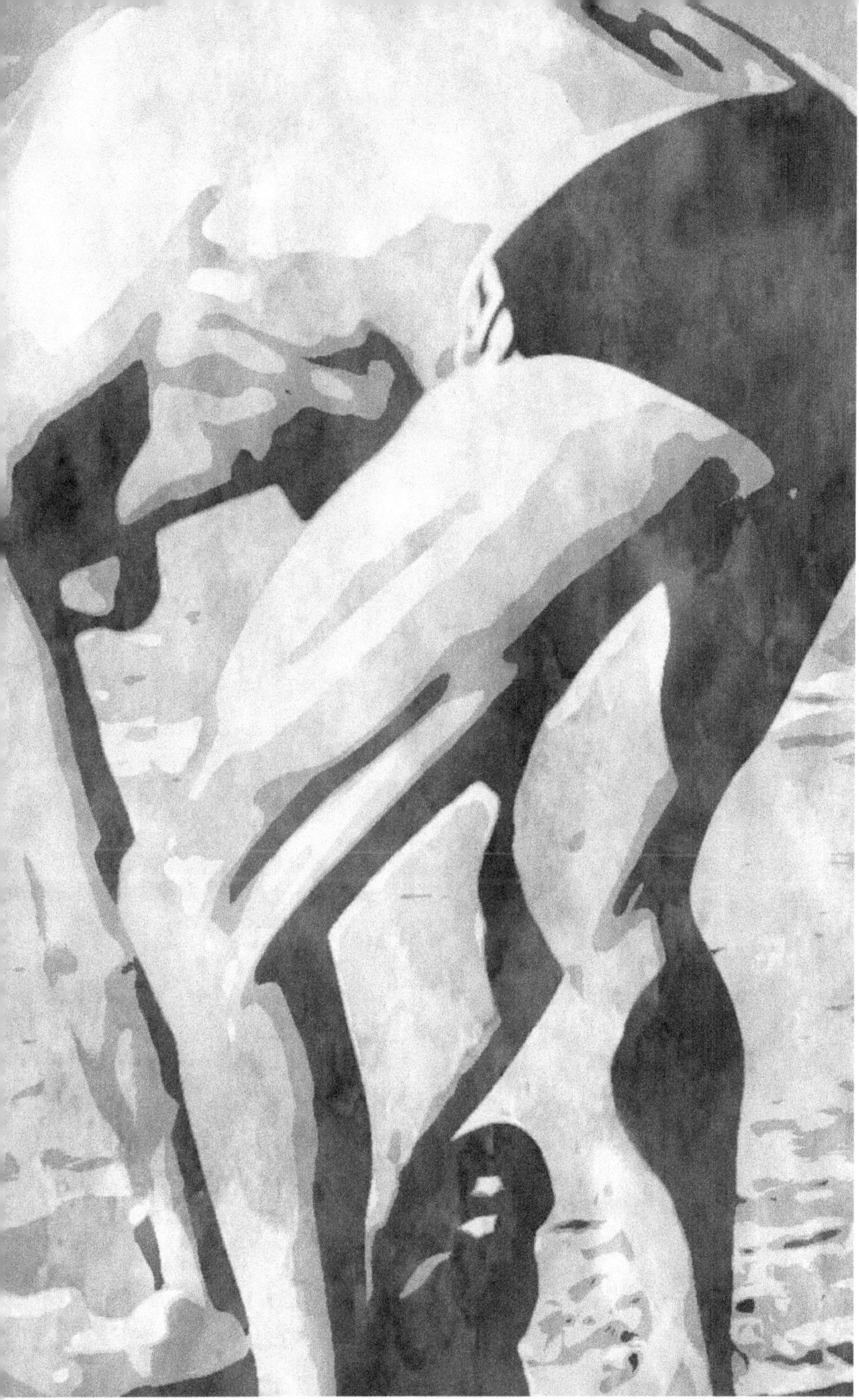

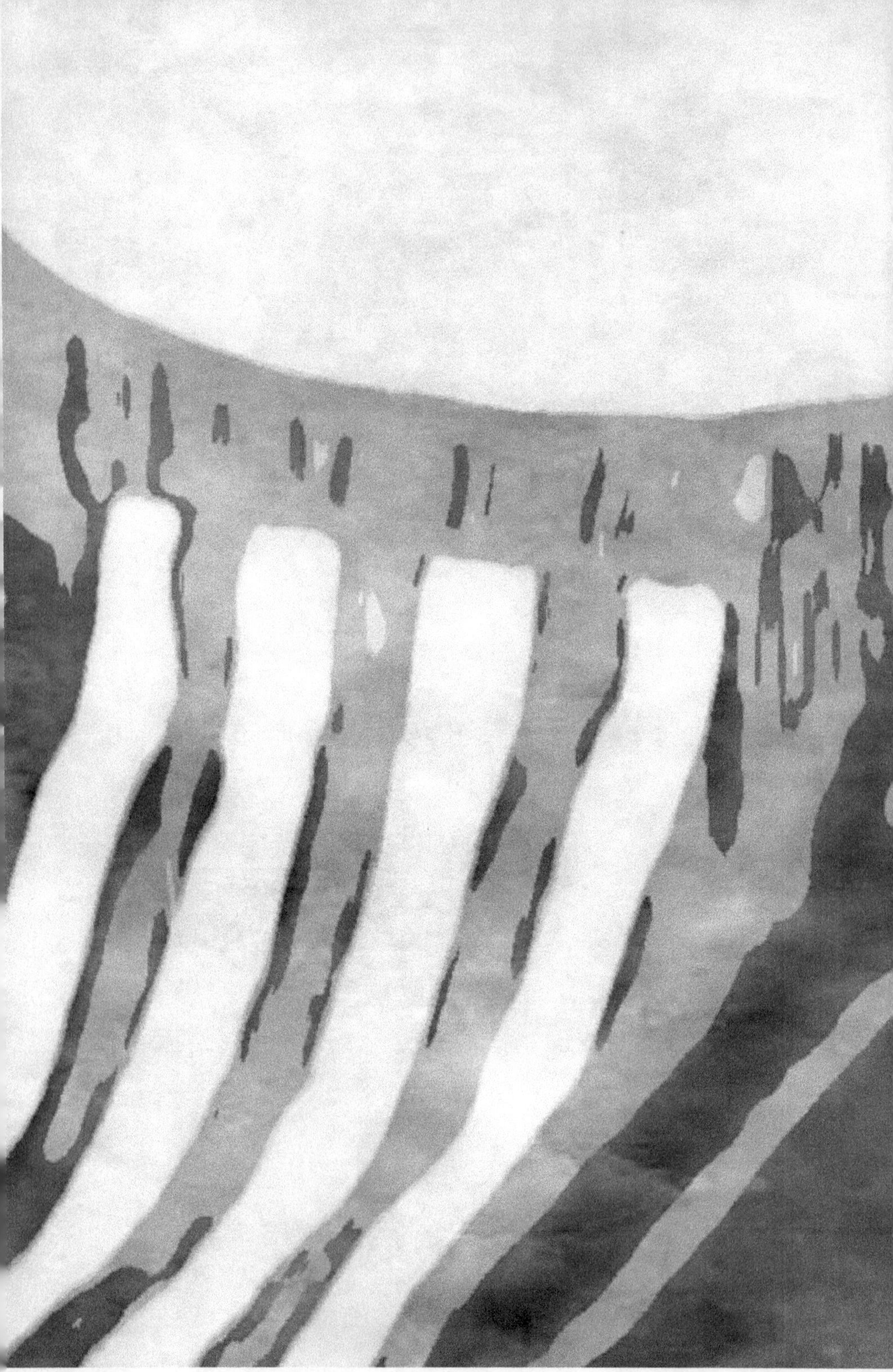

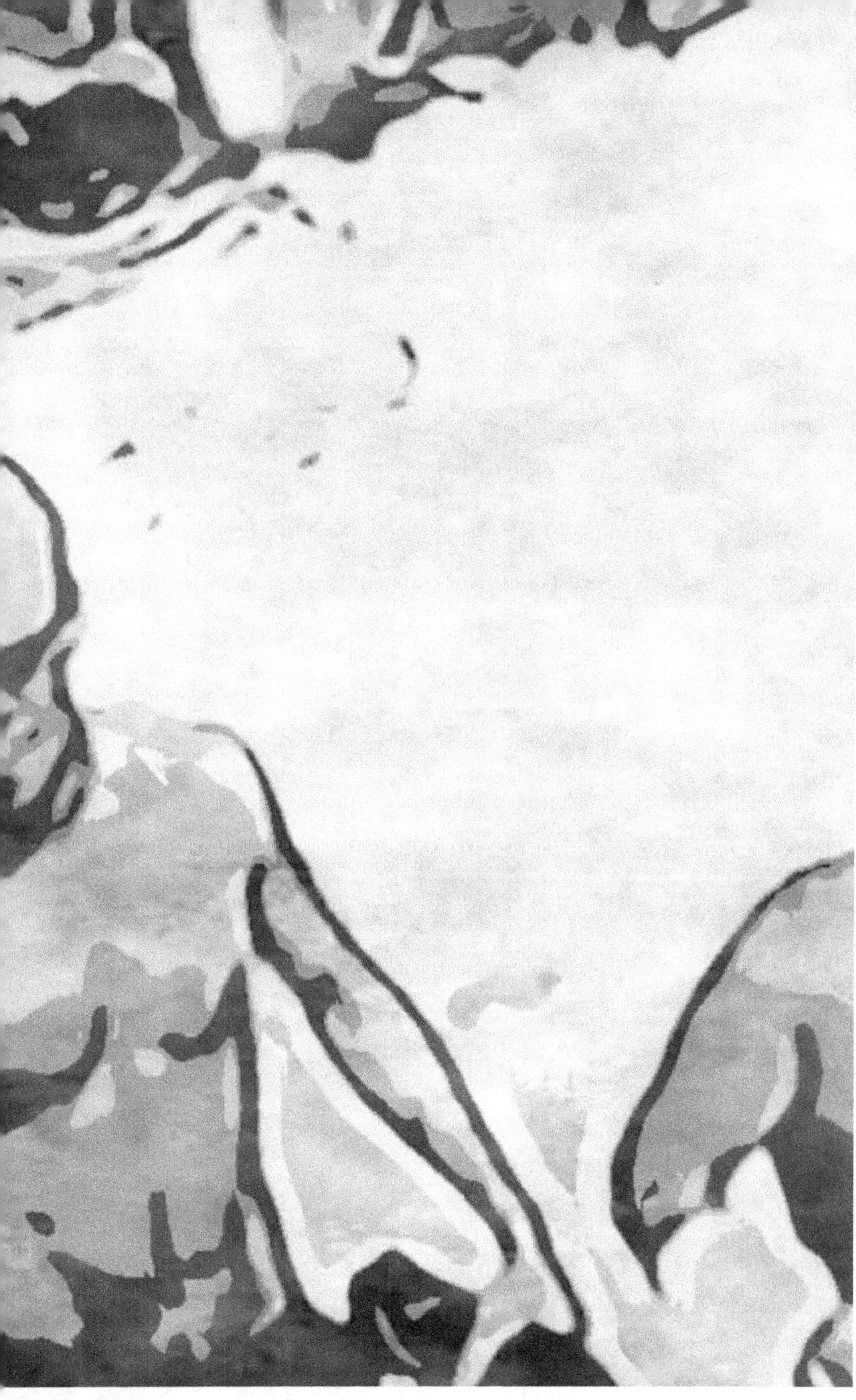

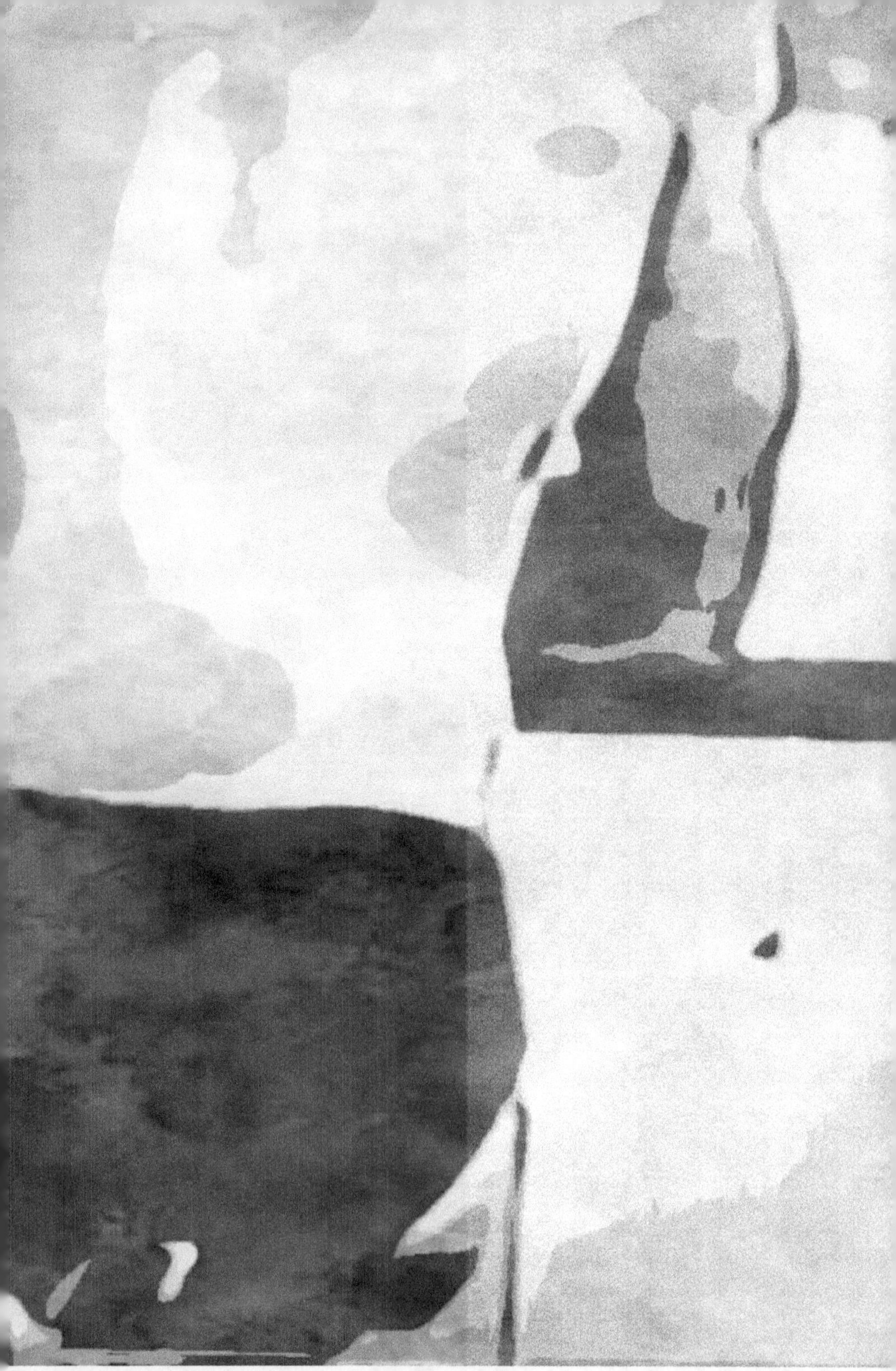

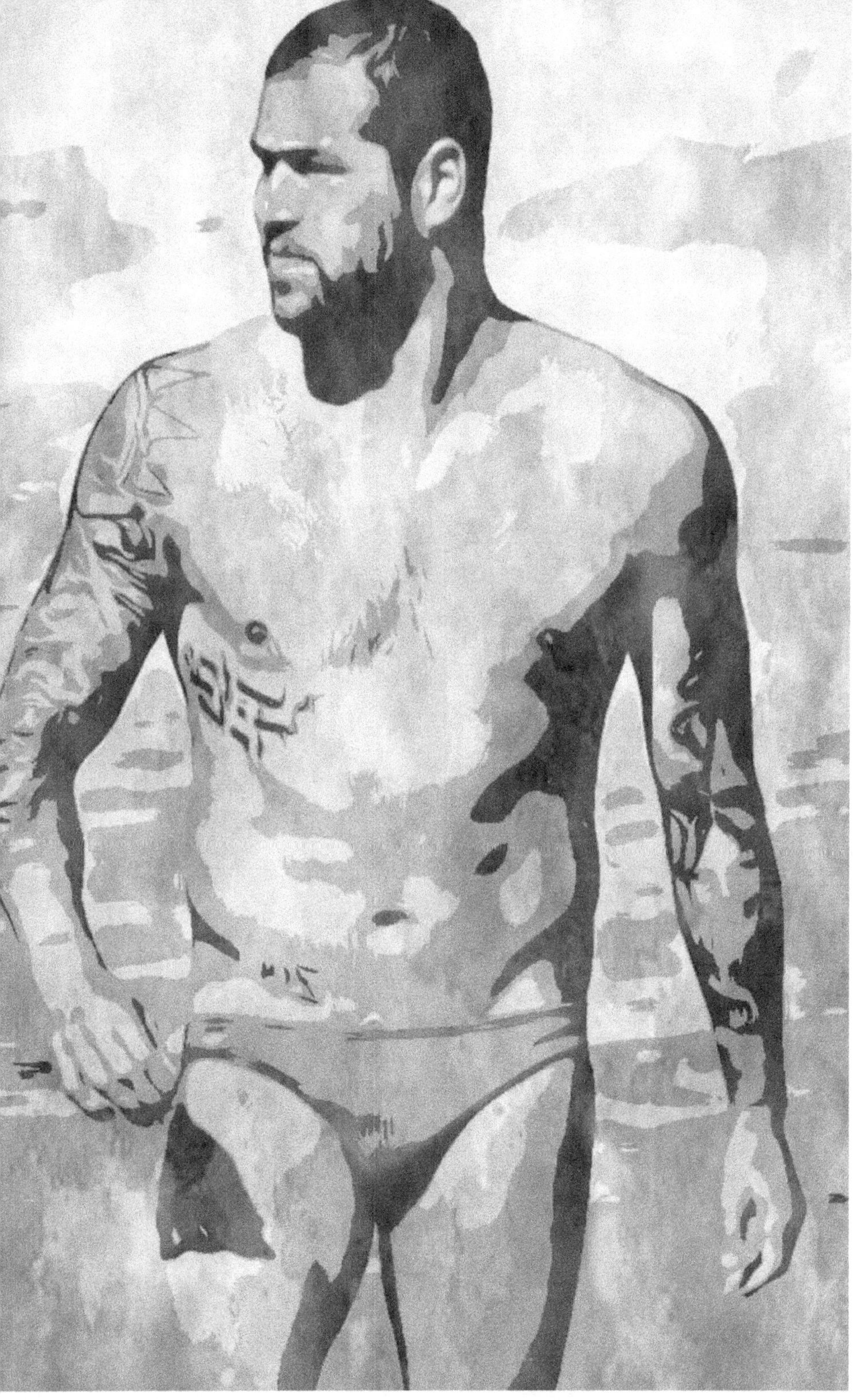

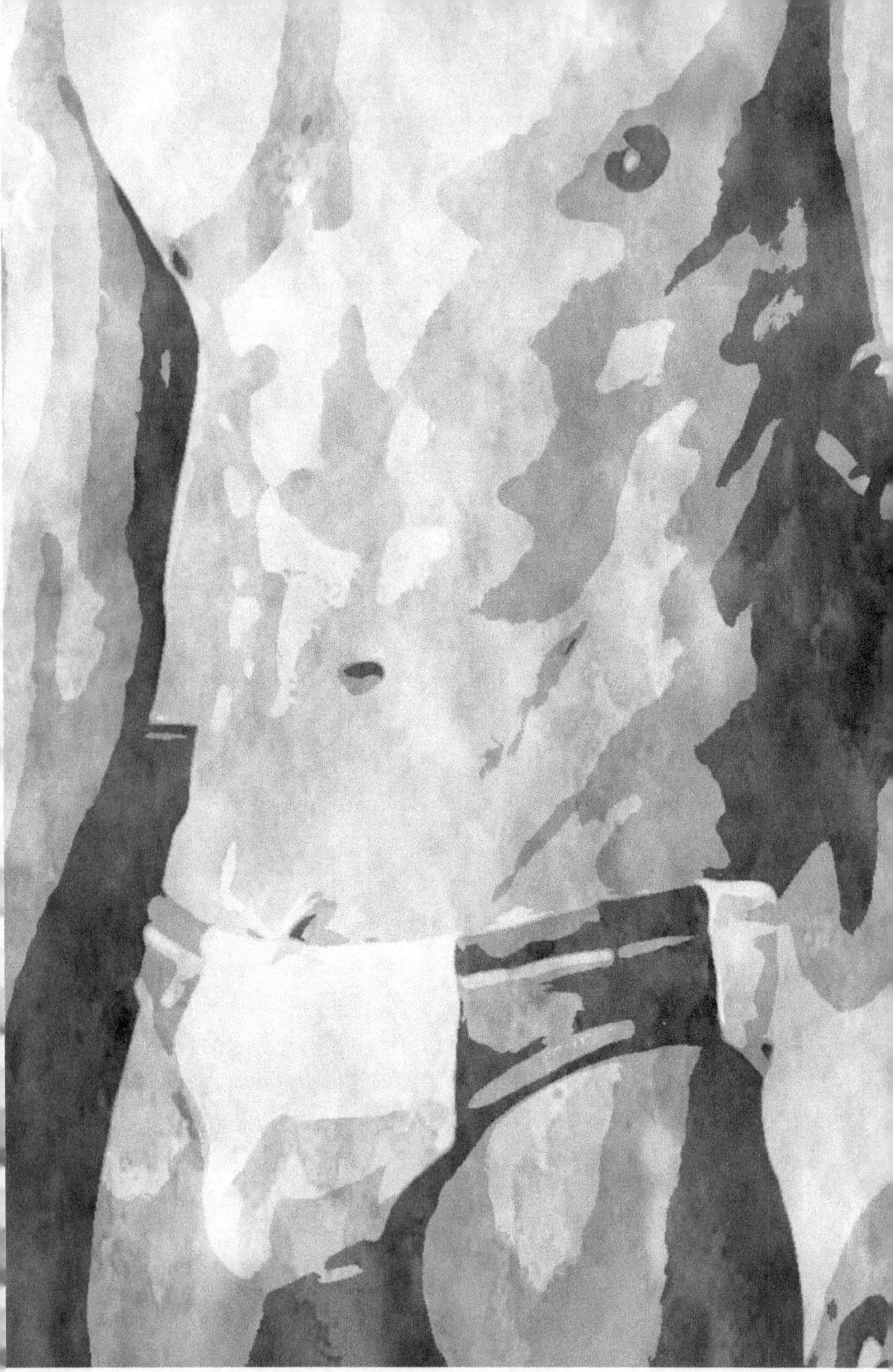

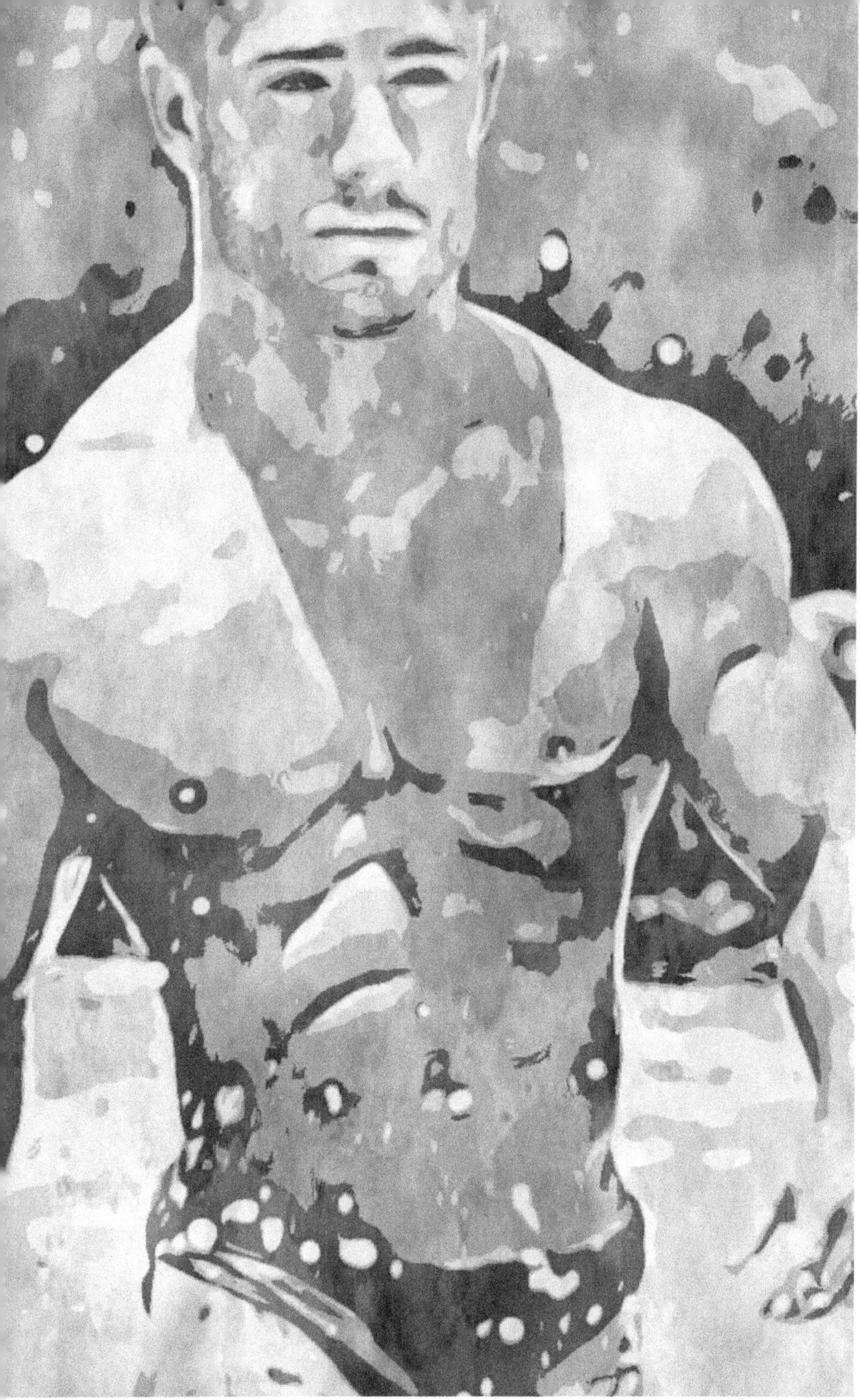

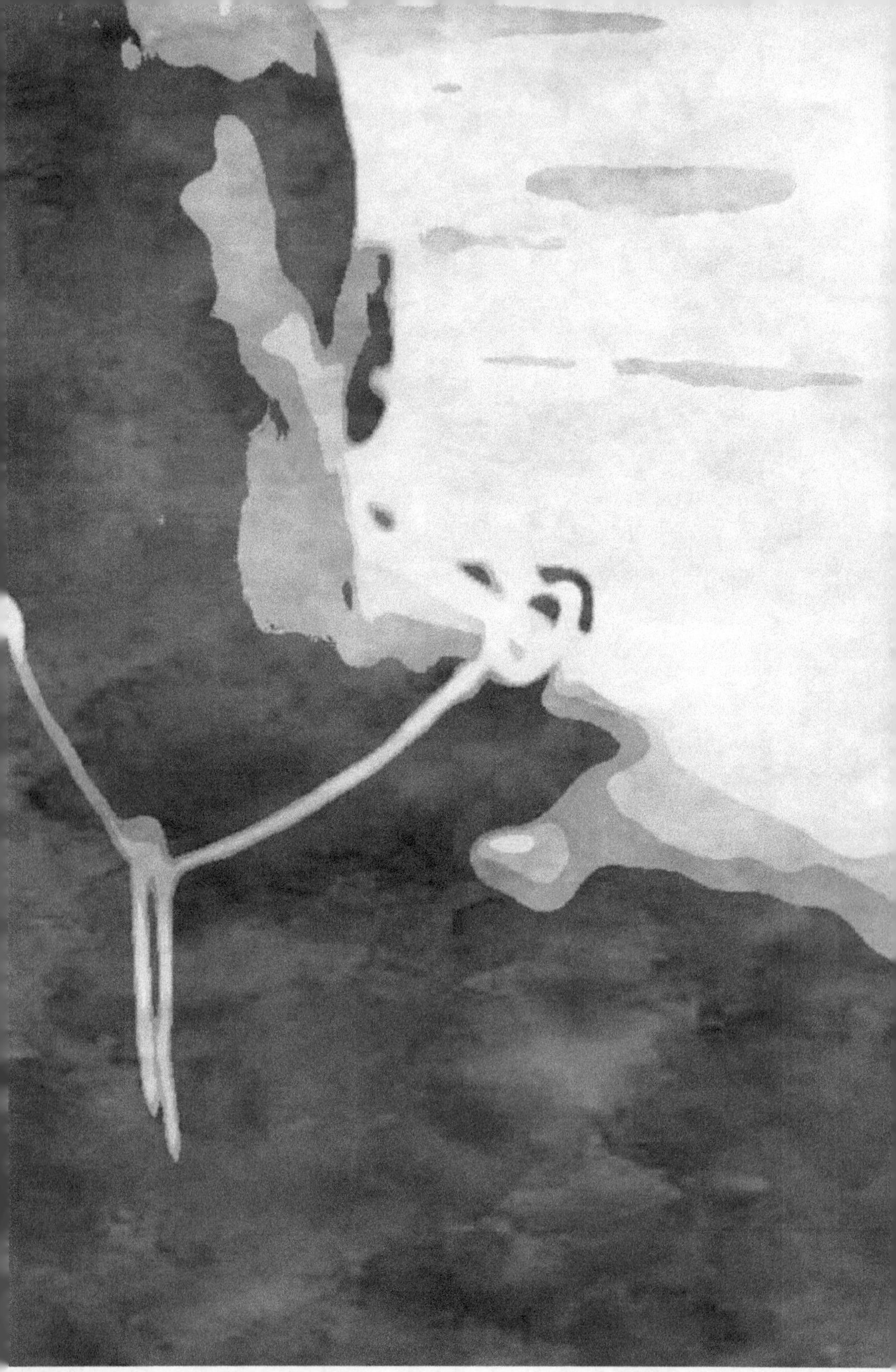

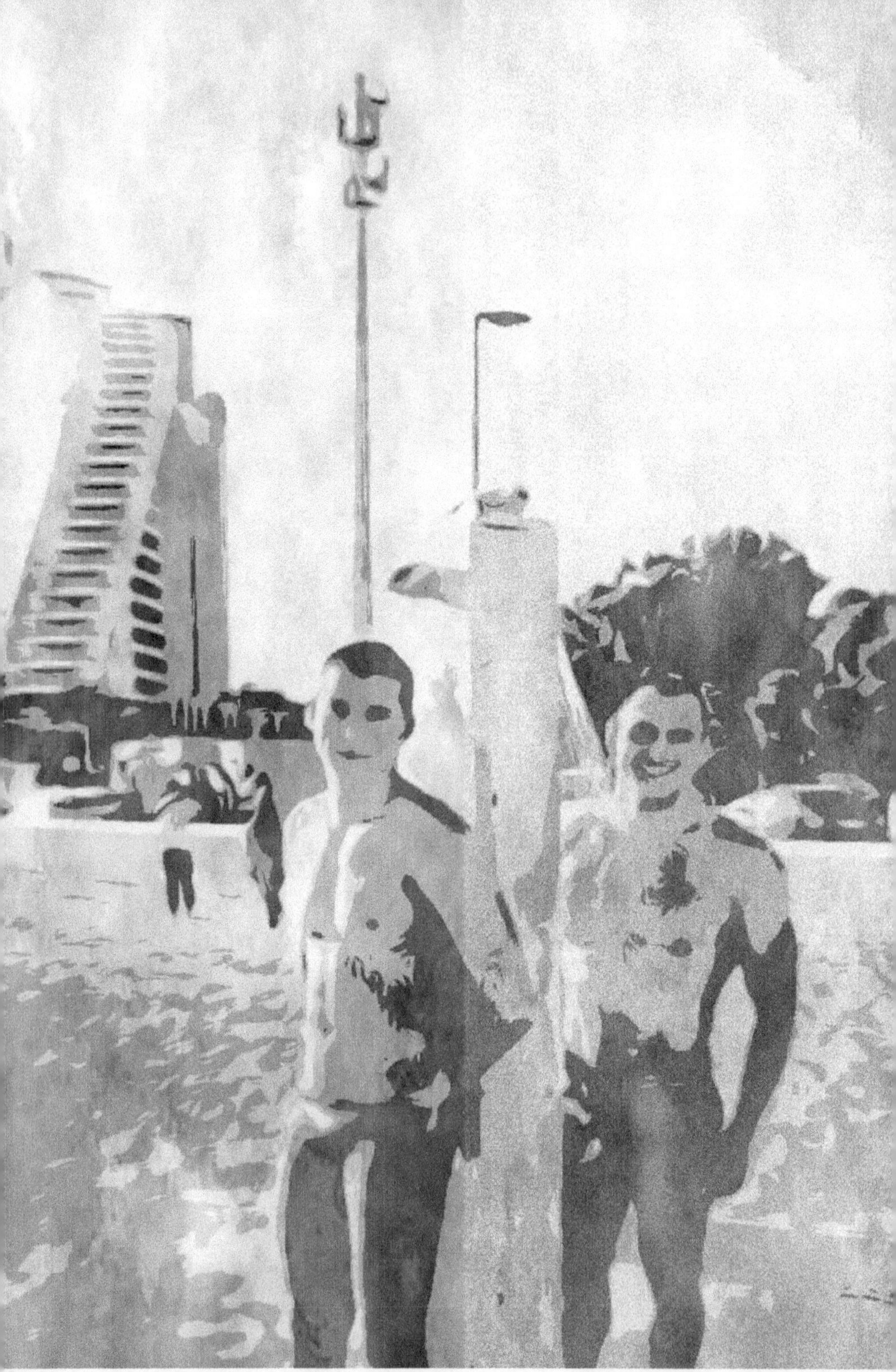

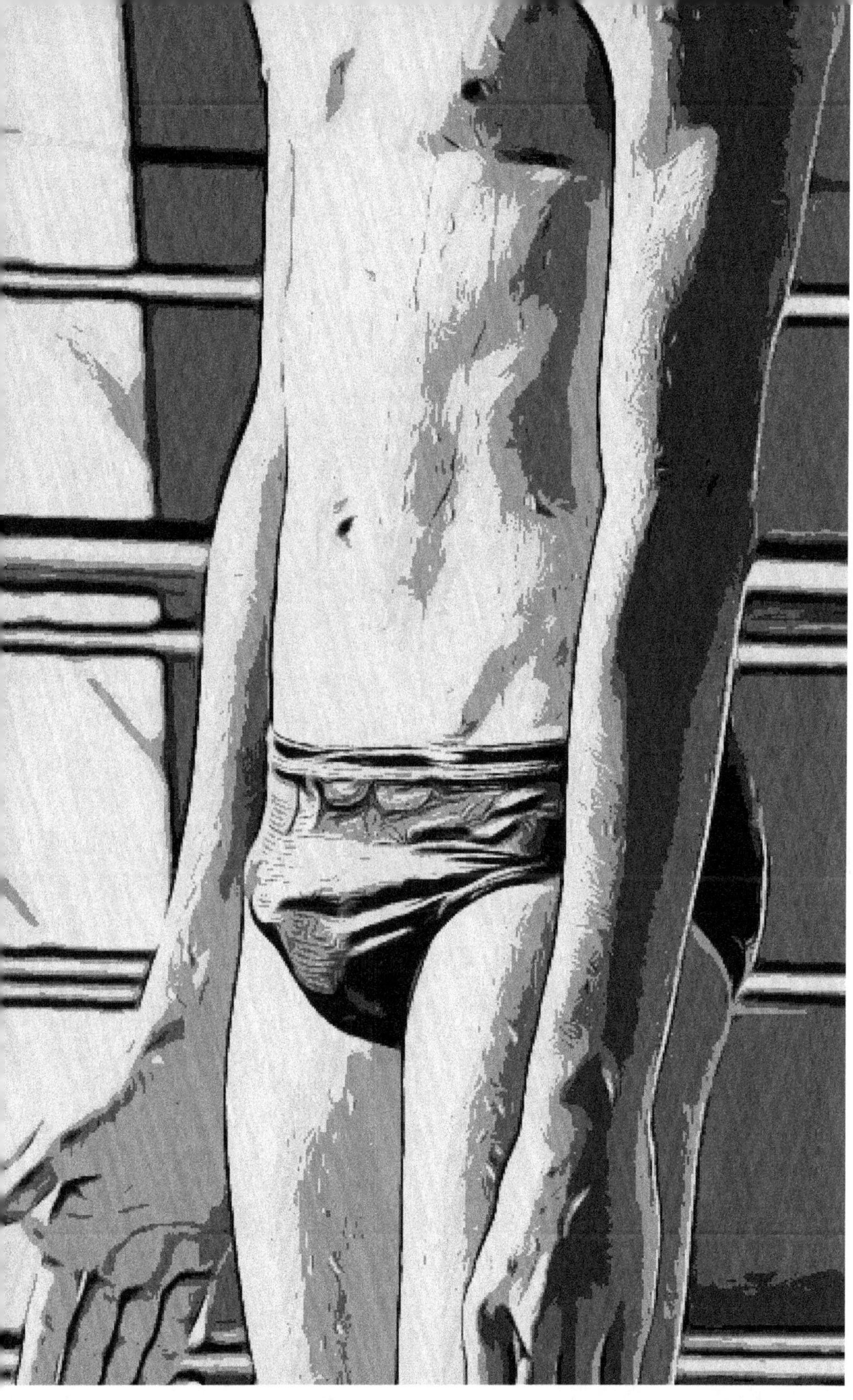

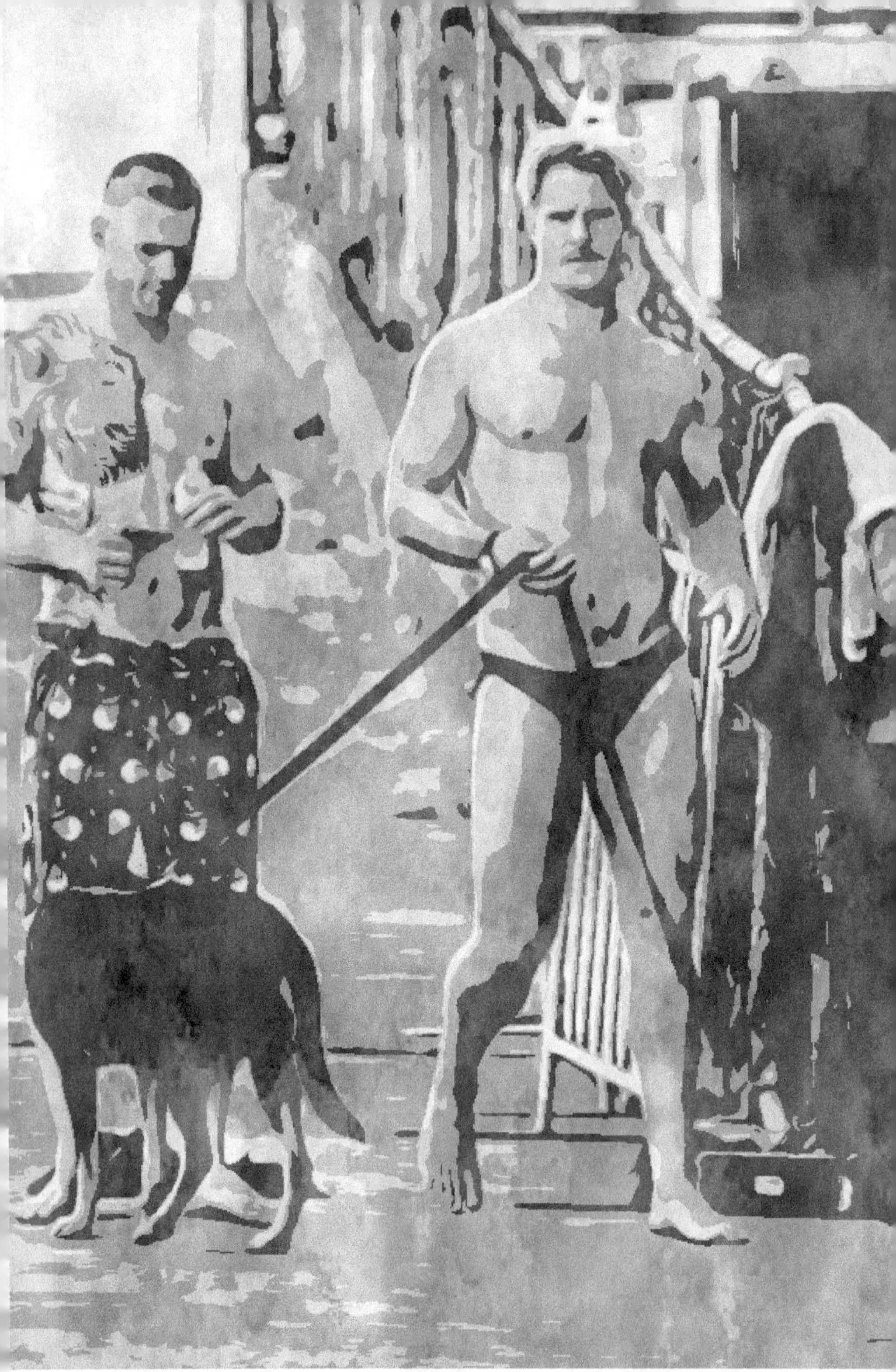

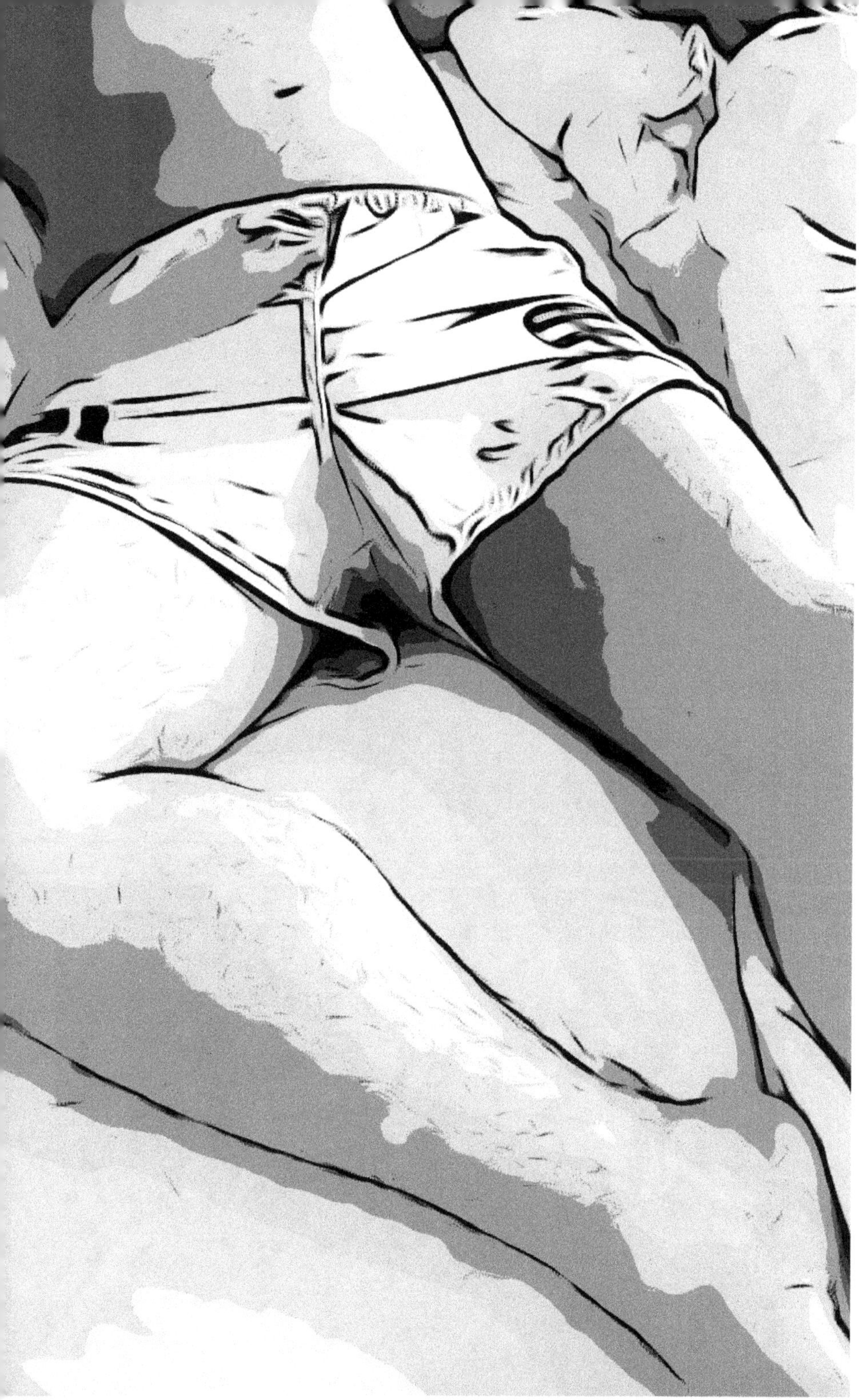

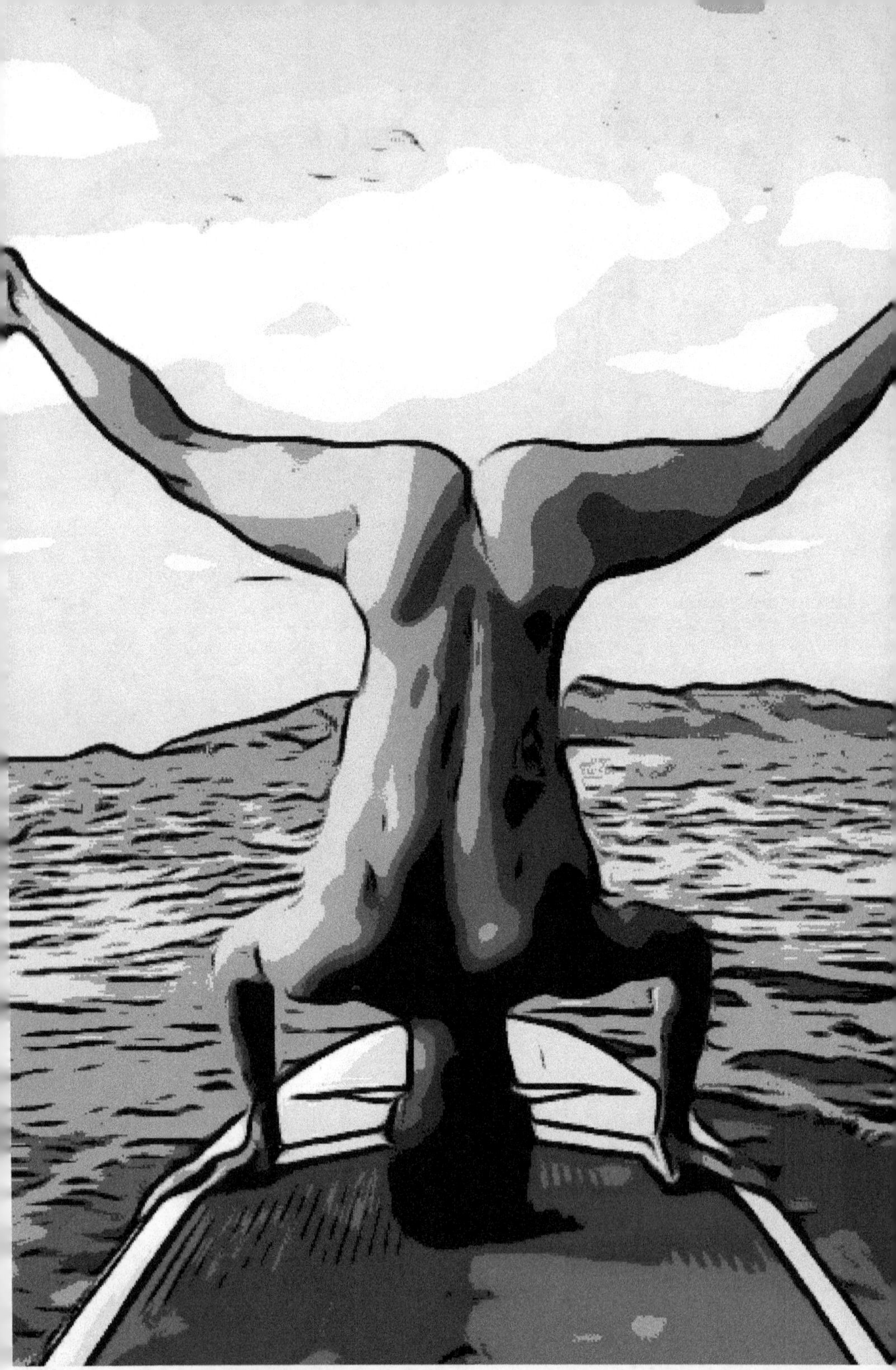

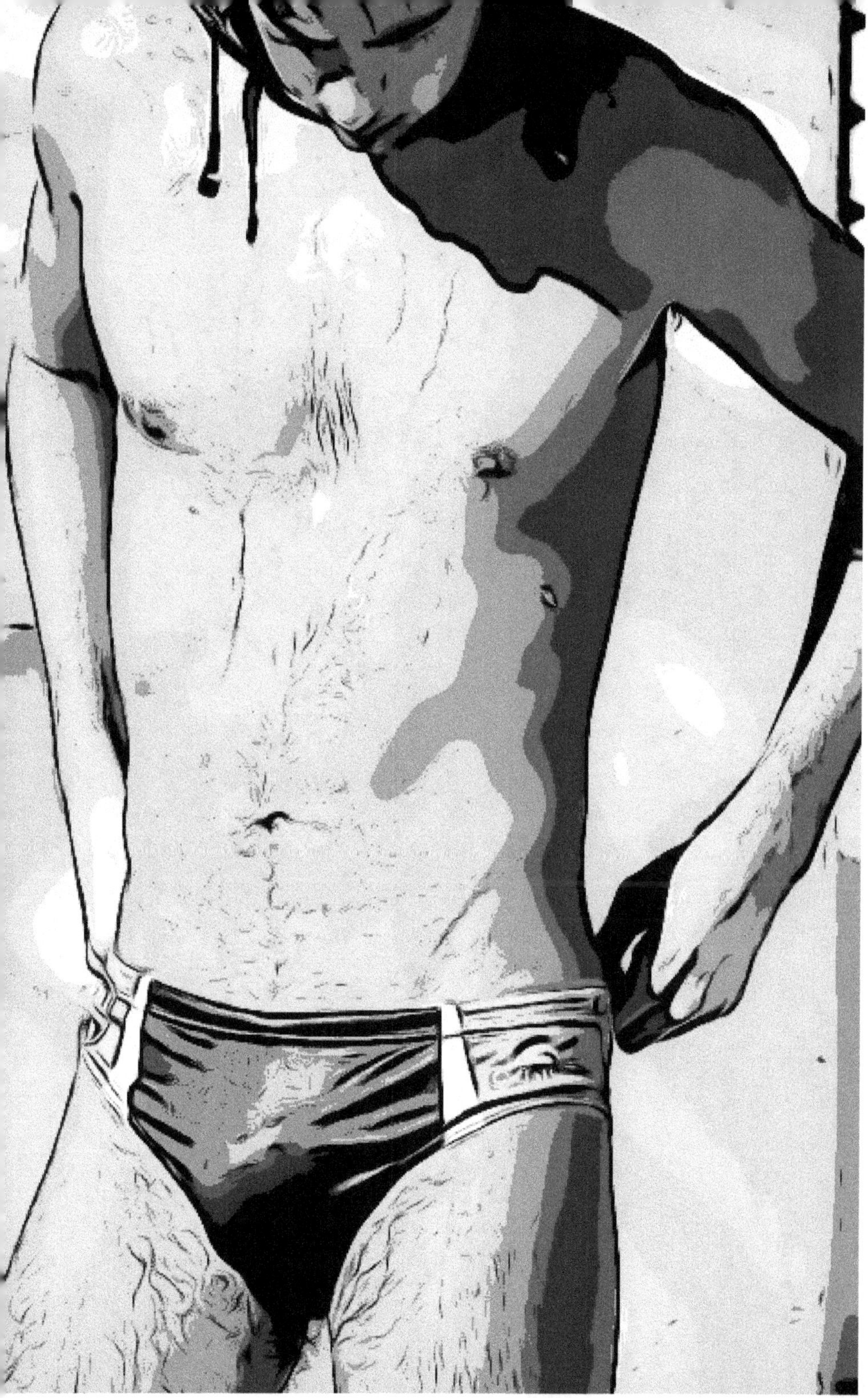

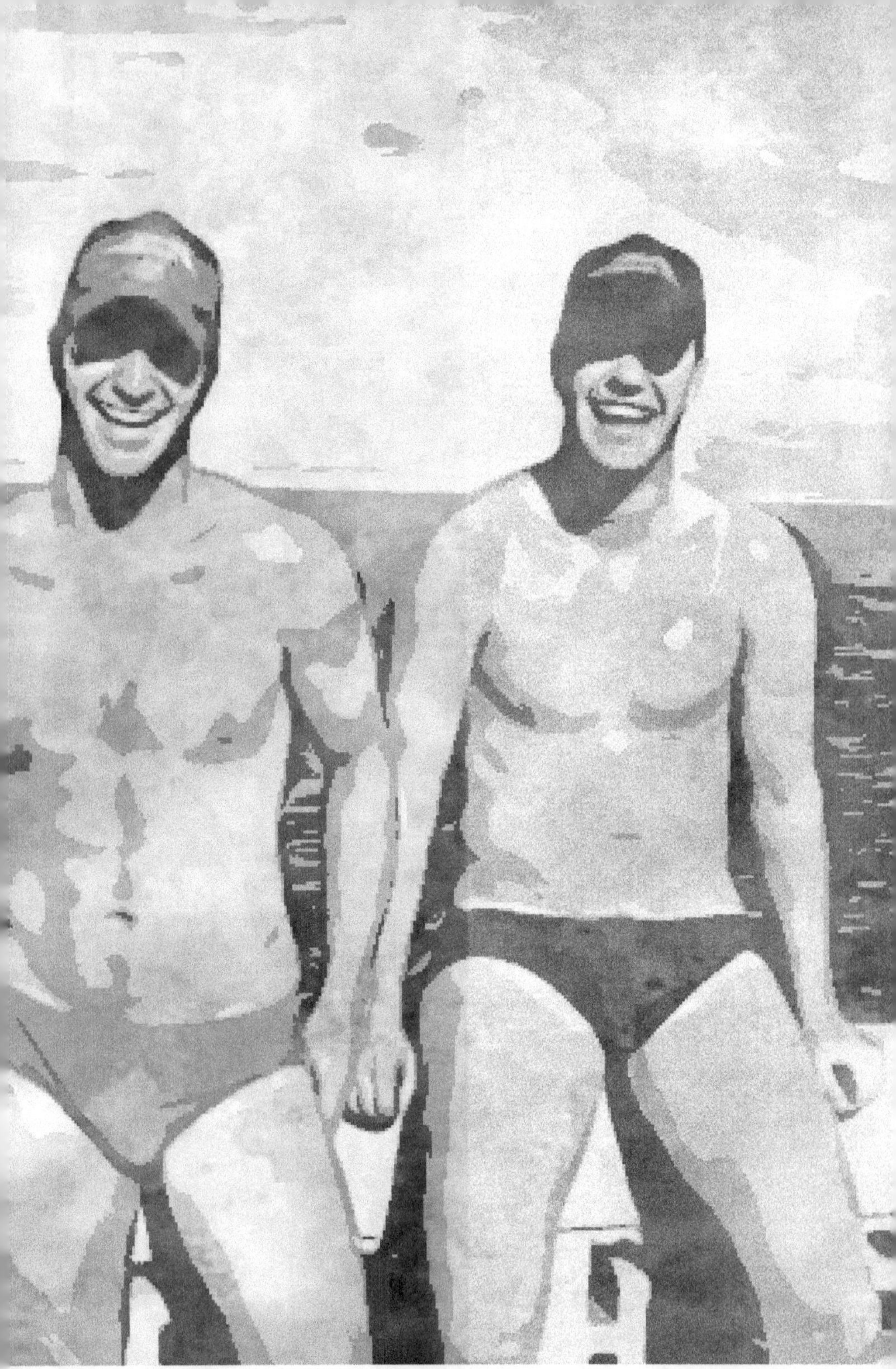

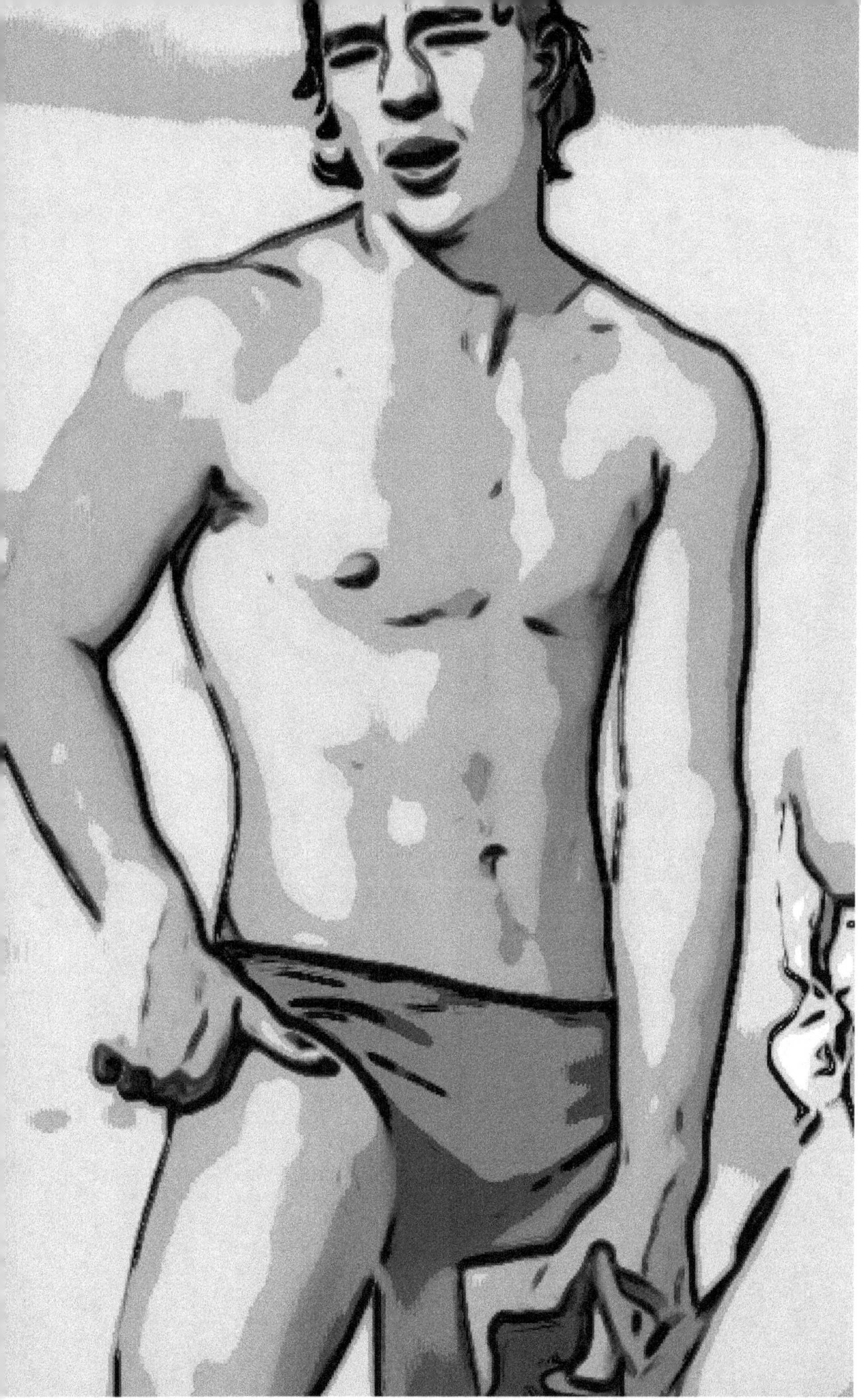

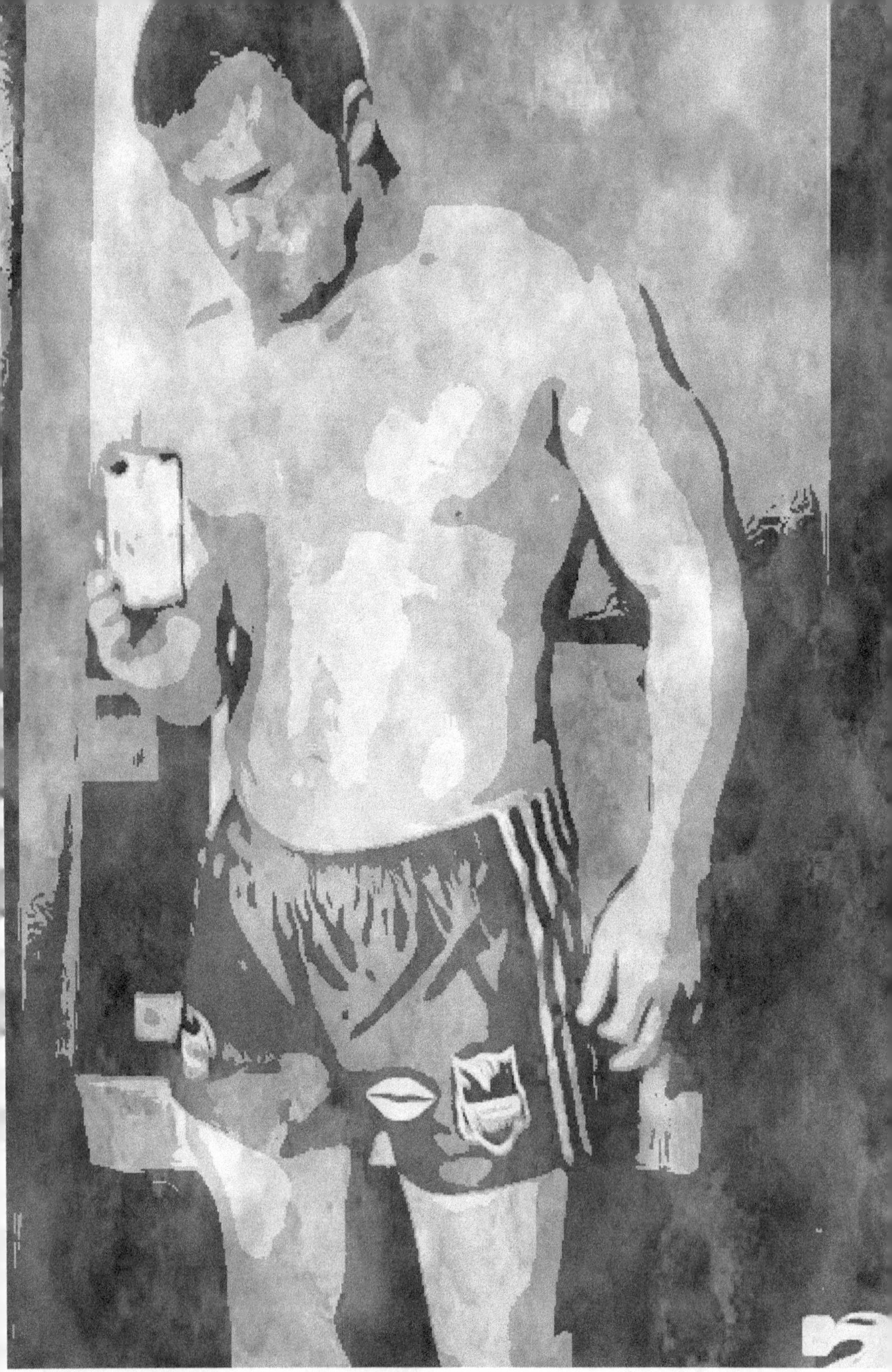

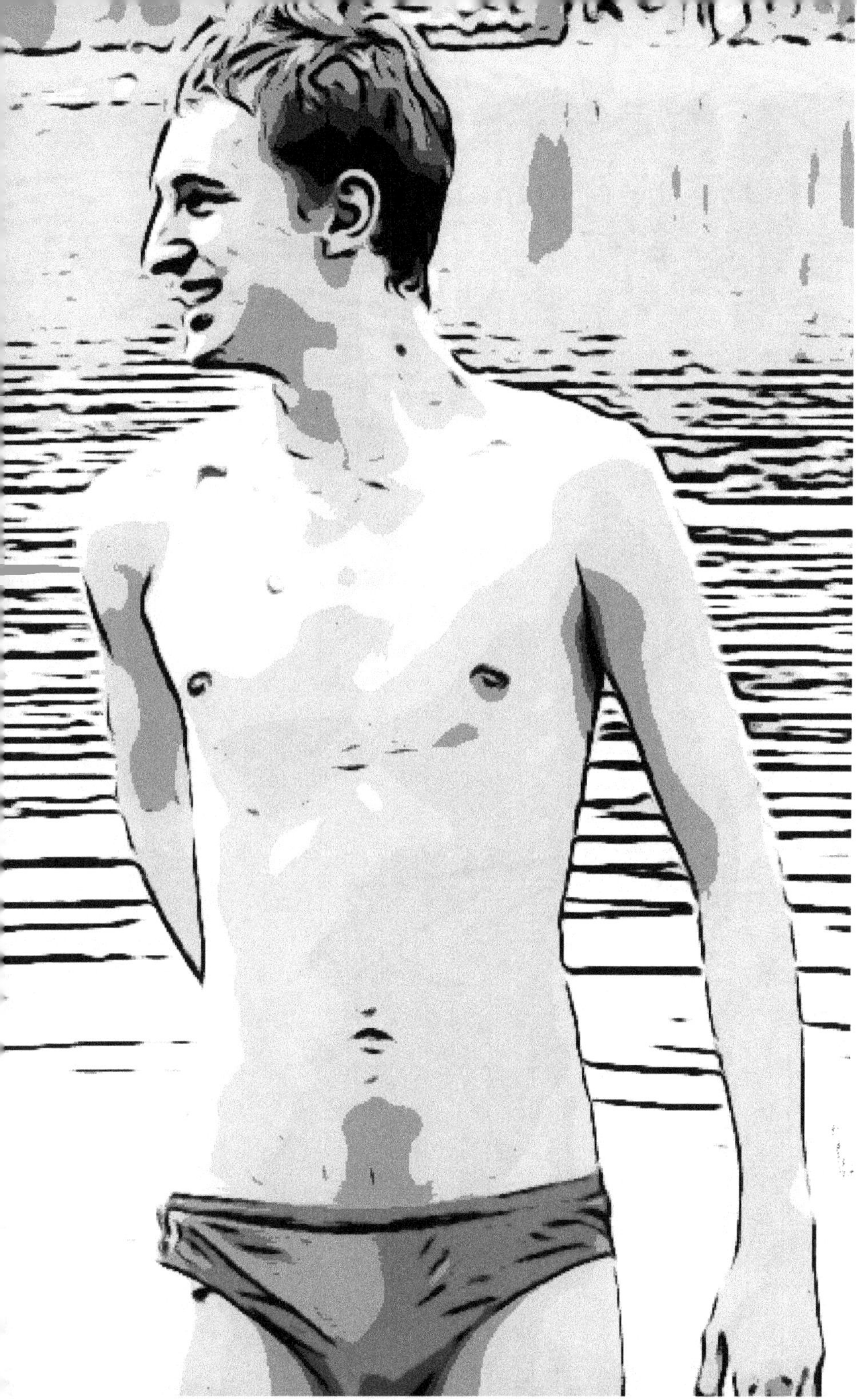

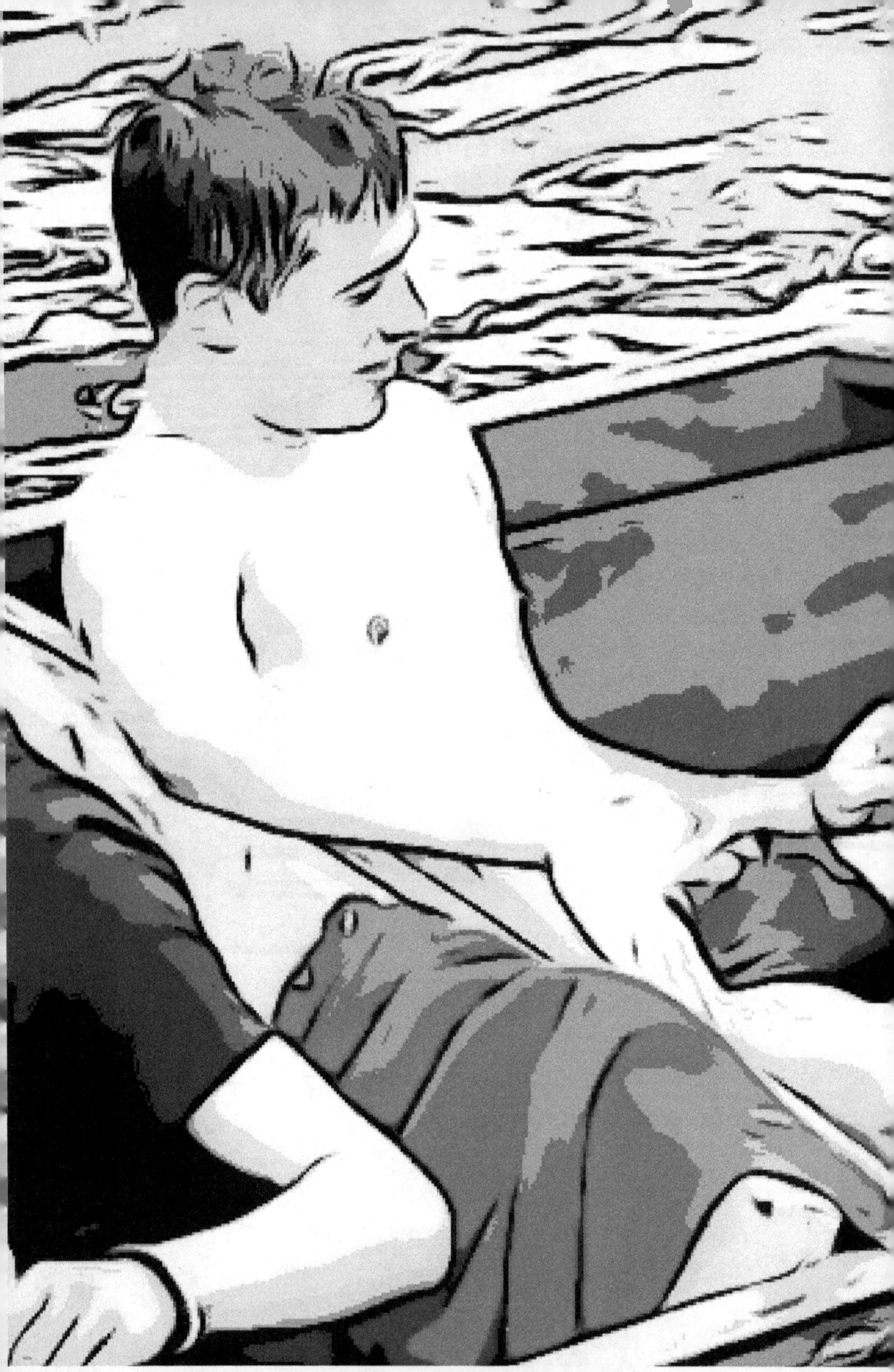

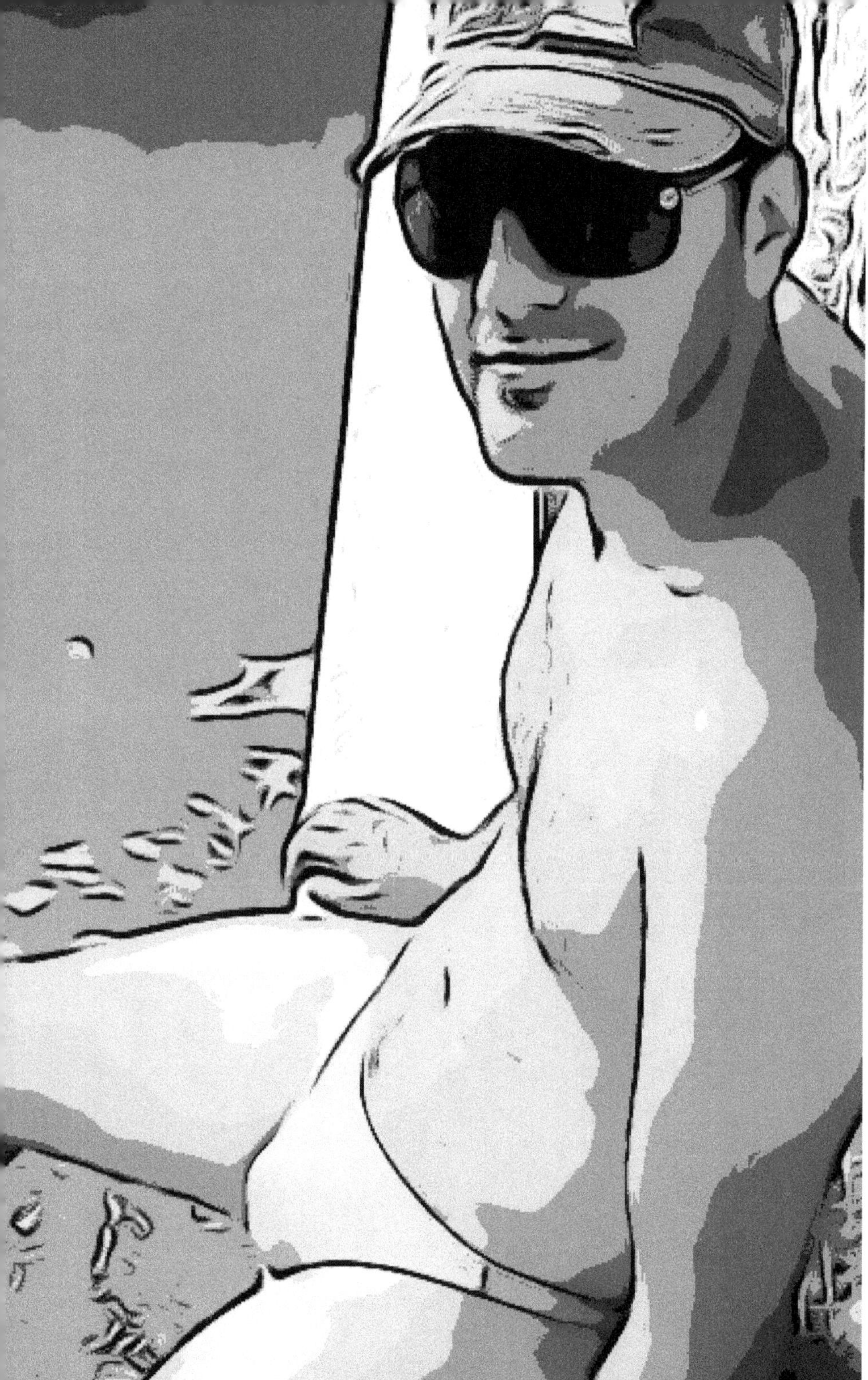

www.ingramcontent.com/pod-product-compliance
Lightning Source LLC
Chambersburg PA
CBHW061226180526
45170CB00003B/1170
* 9 7 8 0 2 4 4 5 5 7 0 5 8 *